The Accounting Function and Management Accounting in Life Insurance Companies

LOMA (Life Office Management Association, Inc.) is an international association founded in 1924. LOMA is committed to a business partnership with its worldwide members in the insurance and financial services industry to improve their management and operations through quality employee development, research, information sharing, and related products and services. Among LOMA's activities is the sponsorship of the FLMI Education Program—an educational program intended primarily for home office and branch office employees.

The ***FLMI Education Program*** consists of two levels—Level I, *Fundamentals of Life and Health Insurance*, and Level II, *Functional Aspects of Life and Health Insurance.* Level I is designed to help students achieve a working knowledge of the life and health insurance business. Level II is designed to provide a more detailed understanding of life and health insurance and related business and management subjects. Students who complete Level I receive a certificate. Students who complete both levels earn the designation Fellow, Life Management Institute (FLMI) and receive a diploma.

Statement of Purpose: LOMA Educational Programs Testing and Designations

Examinations described in the *LOMA Education and Training Catalog* are designed solely to measure whether students have successfully completed the relevant assigned curriculum, and the attainment of the FLMI and other LOMA designations indicates only that all examinations in the given curriculum have been successfully completed. In no way shall a student's completion of a given LOMA course or attainment of the FLMI or other LOMA designation be construed to mean that LOMA in any way certifies that student's competence, training, or ability to perform any given task. LOMA's examinations are to be used solely for general educational purposes, and no other use of the examinations or programs is authorized or intended by LOMA. Furthermore, it is in no way the intention of the LOMA Curriculum and Examinations staff to describe the standard of appropriate conduct in any field of the insurance and financial services industry, and LOMA expressly repudiates any attempt to so use the curriculum and examinations. Any such assessment of student competence or industry standards of conduct should instead be based on independent professional inquiry and the advice of competent professional counsel.

The Accounting Function and Management Accounting in Life Insurance Companies

Elizabeth A. Mulligan, FLMI, ACS, ALHC, AIAA, PAHM

LOMA®
Information That Works
FLMI Education Program
Life Management Institute LOMA
Atlanta, Georgia
www.loma.org

Information in this text may have been changed or updated since its publication date. For current updates, visit www.loma.org.

FLMI 361 Text — The Accounting Function and Management Accounting in Life Insurance Companies

Author:	Elizabeth A. Mulligan, FLMI, ACS, ALHC, AIAA, PAHM
Manuscript Editor:	Susan Conant, FLMI, HIA, CEBS, PAHM
Exam Editor:	Cynthia Mathis Henry, FLMI, ALHC, ACS, PAHM
Project Manager:	Jena L. Kennedy, FLMI, ALHC, ACS, CLU, PAHM
Production Manager:	Michelle Stone Weathers, ACS
Copyeditor and Indexer:	Robert D. Land, FLMI, ACS
Production Coordinator:	Allison Ayers
Print Coordinator:	Amy Souwan
Print Buyer:	Audrey M. Hiers
Permissions Coordinator:	Iris F. Hartley, FLMI, ALHC
Administrative Support:	Mamunah Carter Aurelia K. Hemphill Marion Markus
Cover Design:	Allison Ayers Michelle Stone Weathers, ACS

10 09 08 07 06 05 04 03 02 10 9 8 7 6 5 4 3 2 1

While a great deal of care has been taken to provide accurate, current, and authoritative information in regard to the subject matter covered in this book, the ideas, suggestions, general principles, conclusions, and any other information presented here are for general educational purposes only. This text is sold with the understanding that it is neither designed nor intended to provide the reader with legal, accounting, investment, marketing, or any other types of professional business management advice. If legal advice or other expert assistance is required, the services of a competent professional should be sought.

Library of Congress Cataloging-in-Publication Data

Mulligan, Elizabeth A.
The accounting function and management accounting in life insurance companies/ Elizabeth A. Mulligan.
p. cm.
ISBN 1-57974-148-7
1. Insurance, Life--United States--Accounting. 2. Insurance, Life--Canada--Accounting. 3. Managerial accounting--United States. 4. Managerial accounting--Canada. I. Title.

HG8848.M852 2002
657'.836--dc21 2001038470

ISBN 1-57974-148-7

Printed in the United States of America

Contents

Preface

Many individuals have provided valuable expertise that made this book possible. The membership of LOMA's Education Council, comprised of industry volunteers acting on behalf of the LOMA membership, identifies the membership's most urgent needs in the area of education and directs the LOMA staff to meet those needs. The combined efforts of many highly qualified experts supported the development of *The Accounting Function and Management Accounting in Life Insurance Companies*. On behalf of LOMA and its membership, we would like to express appreciation to those individuals who generously gave their time and energy and shared their considerable expertise for the development of this textbook.

Textbook Development Panel

Because, with permission from the publisher, *The Accounting Function and Management Accounting in Life Insurance Companies* draws heavily upon research originally conducted for a LOMA textbook that preceded it, we first thank the industry experts who served on the textbook development panel for and made enormous contributions to *Accounting and Financial Reporting in Life and Health Insurance Companies,* Elizabeth A. Mulligan and Gene Stone (Atlanta: LOMA, 1997):

- Thomas Allen, CPA, FLMI
- Alan E. Close, CPA, FLMI
- Larry J. Esposito, CPA, FLMI
- Susan I. Flynn, CGA, FLMI, ACS, AIAA
- Jerry Hogya, FLMI
- Laurie Kitchen, CA, FLMI
- Patricia K. London, CPA, FLMI
- Roberta McClellan, FLMI
- Martha A. Meyer, CPA, FLMI
- Steven D. Morris, CPA, FLMI

Textbook Review Panel

On behalf of LOMA, we particularly thank the members of the textbook review panel for *The Accounting Function and Management*

Accounting in Life Insurance Companies. These individuals provided research materials, read and commented on the manuscript, answered many author queries, and provided ideas for ensuring the book's relevance to today's insurance companies. In short, this textbook would have been a very different product without their participation. Their critical judgment, diligence, patience, and technical expertise were essential to the book's accuracy and completeness. These members of the textbook development panel contributed personal time, shared their many years of professional experience and education, and guided the book's focus:

- Jeannie A. Ault, CPA, FLMI, Senior Financial Accounting Analyst, Principal Financial Group
- Lucie Bergeron-Poulin, CMA, FLMI, ACS, Accountant, Industrial-Alliance Life Insurance Company
- Alan E. Close, CPA, FLMI, Associate Controller, Northwestern Mutual Life Insurance Company
- Stephen F. Dolan, CPA, FLMI, ChFC, Senior Assistant Vice President, AMICA Life Insurance Company
- Michael J. Leick, FLMI, Senior Accountant, AEGON USA Realty Advisors, Inc.
- Roberta McClellan, FLMI, Associate Financial Reporting Manager, Great-West Life Assurance Company
- Sherrill A. Nobles, FLMI, ACS, Workflow Supervisor, AEGON USA
- Teresa O'Connor, CGA, Manager, Life Financial Reporting and Planning, Zurich Life Insurance Company of Canada
- Keith Rayburn, FLMI, CLU, ACS, AIRC, HIA, Senior Actuarial Assistant II, J.C. Penney Life Insurance Company

Additional Expert Reviewers

In addition to the members of the textbook review panel, many other individuals contributed their considerable expertise to ensuring the reliability of various specialized aspects of the book.

Several experts reviewed one or more chapters in the early stages of the text's development. For this effort, we owe a debt of gratitude to the following individuals

- Virginia Cook, FLMI, ACS, AIAA, AIRC, Premium Accounting Coordinator, USAble Life
- Lee W. Erickson, FLMI, Manager, Life Financial Reporting, Allmerica Financial Corporation
- Gregory S. Gannon, FLMI, Director—Financial Reporting, American Skandia Life Assurance Company

LOMA Staff and Consultants

All textbooks developed by LOMA are team projects. Many members of LOMA's Education Division staff worked to create this textbook, as did other LOMA staff. The following individuals deserve special mention for the work they performed on this text. Jena L. Kennedy, FLMI, ALHC, ACS, CLU, PAHM, Director, Education & Training, served as project manager. Susan Conant, FLMI, HIA, CEBS, PAHM, Education & Training, served as manuscript editor. Cynthia Mathis Henry, FLMI, ALHC, ACS, PAHM, Senior Associate, Examinations Department, served as examinations editor. Aurelia K. Hemphill, Administrative Assistant III, Education & Training, prepared the glossary and provided administrative support. Mamunah Carter, Administrative Assistant, and Marion Markus, Administrative Specialist, Education & Training, provided additional administrative support.

Audrey M. Hiers, Inventory and Product Sourcing Administrator, Education & Training, provided business support for production of the project. In LOMA's Production Department, Allison Ayers, Production Coordinator II, designed the cover and served as typesetter. Amy Souwan, Production Coordinator II/Print Coordinator, coordinated the printing of the book. LOMA consultant Iris F. Hartley, FLMI, ALHC, obtained permission for use of copyrighted material. Robert D. Land, FLMI, ACS, another LOMA consultant, copyedited the entire manuscript and drafted the index. Also, special thanks to Michelle Stone Weathers, ACS, Manager, Production Department, who moved the project through production.

From the staff of LOMA's Information Center, Olivia Blakemore, ACS, Technical Administrator, Information Center, along with Mallory Eldridge, Writer/Analyst, Information Center, and Janet

Smith, Information Center Researcher, frequently assisted with research for the project.

And finally, thanks to William H. Rabel, Ph.D., FLMI, CLU, Senior Vice President, Education Division, for his encouragement and support throughout the text's development.

Elizabeth A. Mulligan, FLMI, ACS, ALHC, AIAA, PAHM
Atlanta, Georgia
2002

Introduction

The Accounting Function and Management Accounting in Life Insurance introduces students to essential accounting activities that virtually all insurers undertake, including management accounting and budgeting.

This book has been designed for students who are preparing for the FLMI 361 examination, which is part of the Fellow, Life Management Institute (FLMI) designation program. Several features have been included in each chapter to help you organize your studies, reinforce your understanding of the materials, and prepare for the examination. As we describe each of these features, we give you suggestions for studying the material.

- **Learning Objectives.** The first page of each chapter contains a list of learning objectives to help you focus your studies. Before reading each chapter, review these learning objectives. Then, as you read the chapter, look for material that will help you meet the learning objectives.

- **Chapter Outline.** The first page of each chapter contains an outline of the chapter. Review this outline to gain an overview of the material that will be covered; then scan through the chapter to familiarize yourself with the presentation of the information. By looking at the headings and figures, you will get a preview of how the various subjects relate to each other.

- **Key Terms.** The key terms and concepts associated with insurance administration are reviewed and explained in this text. All of the important terminology introduced in this text is defined or explained when it is first used. Important terminology is highlighted with ***bold italic type*** when the term is first defined and is included in a list of key terms at the end of each chapter. All key terms also appear in a comprehensive glossary at the end of the book. As you read each chapter, pay special attention to these key terms.

- **Figures.** Figures appear throughout the text and are designed to illustrate or give examples of the text's discussions of selected important topics. Note that information contained in figures may be tested on FLMI Program examination.

- **Insights.** Insights may appear throughout the text and are designed to amplify the text's descriptions of certain topics. These insights should help you get a better feel for the functional areas and activities involved in insurance administration. Information contained in insights may be tested on the examinations for this course and other LOMA courses.

- **Glossary.** A comprehensive glossary containing definitions of all key terms appears at the end of the book. Each glossary entry indicates in which chapter a key term is discussed. The glossary includes references to important equivalent terms, acronyms, and contrasting terms or concepts.

Using LOMA Study Aids

LOMA has prepared study aids designed to help students prepare for the Course FLMI 361 examination. LOMA recommends that you use all of the study aids available for this course. **Studies indicate that students who use LOMA study aids consistently perform significantly better on LOMA examinations than students who do not use these study aids.**

Using the Prep Pak for This Course

In addition to this book, LOMA's *Prep Pak for FLMI 361* is assigned reading for students preparing for the FLMI Program examination. Used along with this textbook, the Prep Pak will help you master the course material. The Prep Pak includes chapter review exercises, practice exam questions, a full-scale sample examination in both paper and electronic format, and answers to every question in the Prep Pak.

The *Prep Pak* may be revised periodically. To ensure that you are studying from the correct texts, check the current *LOMA Education and Training Catalog* for a description of the texts assigned for the examination for which you are preparing.

Finally, course instructors should know that LOMA has prepared an *Instructor's Kit for FLMI 361*, designed to help company instructors prepare to teach preparatory classes for the FLMI 361 examination.

Suggested LOMA Study Aids

Some students may find it helpful to undertake a quick review of material related to this course in the LOMA *StepOne Series* publication:

- *Intro to Insurance Company Accounting* (1999) provides an overview of the accounting concepts that you might encounter in studying *The Accounting Function and Management Accounting in Life Insurance Companies.*

Chapter 1

Accounting Information

Chapter Outline

Definition and Purpose of Accounting

Users of Accounting Information
- Internal Users
- External Users

Fields of Accounting
- Financial Accounting
- Management Accounting

The Accounting Function
- Public Accounting
- Private Accounting

Accounting Regulation in the United States
- National Association of Insurance Commissioners
- Internal Revenue Service
- American Institute of Certified Public Accountants
- Securities and Exchange Commission
- Financial Accounting Standards Board

Accounting Regulation in Canada
- Office of the Superintendent of Financial Institutions
- Canada Customs and Revenue Agency
- Canadian Institute of Chartered Accountants

Course Overview

OBJECTIVES

After reading this chapter, you should be able to

- Define *accounting* and recognize why the accounting function is critical to life insurance companies
- Identify the key users and uses of accounting information
- Distinguish between financial accounting and management accounting
- Distinguish between generally accepted accounting principles (GAAP) and statutory accounting practices in the United States
- Recognize the roles of various governmental and professional organizations in the regulation of accounting and financial reporting in the United States and Canada

Each of us needs to have a basic understanding of accounting and financial reporting because we all contribute to the success of our employers, as well as that of the financial services industry as a whole. A basic knowledge of accounting can improve our ability to make the types of important decisions that are required in today's business environment. The more we know about the potential impact a particular decision may have on our company's financial position, the better prepared we are to make the best decision. Knowledge of accounting also helps us to make informed financial decisions.

In this chapter, we introduce the subject of accounting and financial reporting for life insurance companies. We describe the uses and users of accounting information and the different types of accounting required to meet the diverse needs of these users. Chapter 1 also discusses accounting regulations, particularly as they apply to life insurance companies in the United States and Canada.

Definition and Purpose of Accounting

Forecasting and monitoring the financial impact of a company's decisions are the purposes of the accounting function. By definition, ***accounting*** is a system or set of rules and methods for collecting, recording, summarizing, reporting, and analyzing financial information. Accounting provides an established system for categorizing, measuring, and monitoring the financial condition and performance of a company as well as segments, product lines, or divisions within the company. The accounting function consists of processes and activities that help to answer five key business questions, which are summarized in Figure 1-1.

To provide answers to these key business questions, the accounting function monitors and measures financial transactions. A ***financial transaction*** is a business transaction to which a company must assign an objective monetary value, whether the impact on the company is large or small, actual or expected. Virtually all business transactions are financial in nature, because they involve either a transfer of funds or the promise of a transfer of funds or some other resource that has monetary value.

The answers to the questions in Figure 1-1 directly affect a company's key financial goals: solvency and profitability. Generally, a company is *solvent* if it owns more than it owes; a company is *profitable* if it earns more than it spends. Specifically, ***solvency*** is the ability of a

FIGURE 1-1. Five Key Business Questions.

- **What does the company own?**
- **What does the company owe?**
- **What has the company earned?**
- **What has the company spent?**
- **What has the company retained?**

company to meet its financial obligations as they come due. ***Profitability*** is the degree to which a company is successful in consistently generating money for its owners. Because solvency and profitability are key to a company's success, accounting activities affect everyone's job—including yours—whether you work in the accounting function or in another area of your company.

Users of Accounting Information

Many people and organizations rely on the financial information contained in a company's accounting records and reports. Accounting information generally is designed to meet the needs of one of two groups of these interested parties: internal users and external users.

Internal Users

Generally, internal users are people inside a company who make decisions that affect the company's operations, such as the company's directors, officers, and managers. Internal users of accounting information also include company employees whose performance can be enhanced by an understanding of the company's financial position or operations. Internal users of a company's financial information typically have a direct financial interest in that information because they can gain or lose money as a result of the company's financial performance.

External Users

External users of accounting information are people outside a company who use the company's financial information to make personal, investment, or regulatory decisions about the company. External users of a company's financial information may have either a direct or an indirect financial interest in the company's performance. A person or an organization that can gain or lose money as a result of a company's financial performance is said to have a direct financial interest in the company. External users who have a direct financial interest include an insurer's individual and group policyowners, beneficiaries, and insureds; stockholders and potential investors; outside agents and brokers; and creditors.

Other external users of a company's financial information—including competing companies, federal agencies, state and provincial insurance departments or commissioners that oversee insurers' operations, independent rating agencies, and tax authorities—typically have an indirect interest in the company's financial information. Generally, an indirect financial interest means that the person or organization seeking a company's financial information is doing so on behalf of other organizations or people, who may or may not have a direct financial interest in the company's performance.

The distinction between an insurer's internal and external users is often blurred because many insurance company employees are also company policyowners, insureds, or stockholders. As such, these employees are both internal and external users of the insurer's financial information. In addition, the distinction between a direct and indirect financial interest in a company may also overlap. For example, an insurance regulator may have an indirect financial interest in a life insurance company. However, if the regulator is also a policyowner of that company, then he or she also has a direct financial interest in the company.

Fields of Accounting

The various fields of accounting were developed in response to the diverse needs of interested users of a company's financial information. All accounting systems are designed to provide reliable, precise, and consistent tracking and reporting of financial information. However, different fields of accounting provide different types of financial information. Keep in mind that different users of financial information need to answer different questions as they analyze a company's financial information. Consequently, the various fields of accounting have emerged to fit the varied interests of these diverse users. The two major fields of accounting are financial accounting and management accounting.

Financial Accounting

Financial accounting focuses primarily on reporting a company's financial information to meet the needs of the company's external users. Using financial accounting, a company communicates summarized results of numerous transactions, typically through financial statements. ***Financial statements*** are standardized reports of a company's major monetary events and transactions. Common financial statements that insurers use include the

- ***Balance sheet:*** a financial statement that shows an insurer's financial condition or position as of a specified date
- ***Income statement:*** a financial statement that reports an insurer's profits or losses by summarizing the insurer's revenues and expenses during a specified period
- ***Cash flow statement:*** a financial statement that provides information about an insurer's cash receipts (inflows) and cash disbursements (outflows) during a specified period
- ***Statement of owners' equity:*** a financial statement that shows the changes that occurred in an insurer's stockholders' or policyowners' equity during a specified period

In addition, notes and supplementary information, which usually accompany an insurer's financial statements, disclose other important transactions and activities that occurred during the period. Figure 1-2 shows how a company's balance sheet and income statement help to answer the five key business questions listed in Figure 1-1. You can see samples of a life insurance company's financial statements on the CD-ROM that accompanies this course.

A company's financial statements focus on the company's historical financial information. Also, financial statements must conform to applicable laws, regulations, and accounting standards. In the following sections, we describe the key accounting standards associated with financial accounting for life insurers in the United States and Canada.

Generally Accepted Accounting Principles—United States and Canada

Generally accepted accounting principles (GAAP) are a set of financial accounting standards that all public companies in the United States and all companies in Canada follow when preparing their

FIGURE 1-2. Financial Statements Answer Five Key Business Questions.

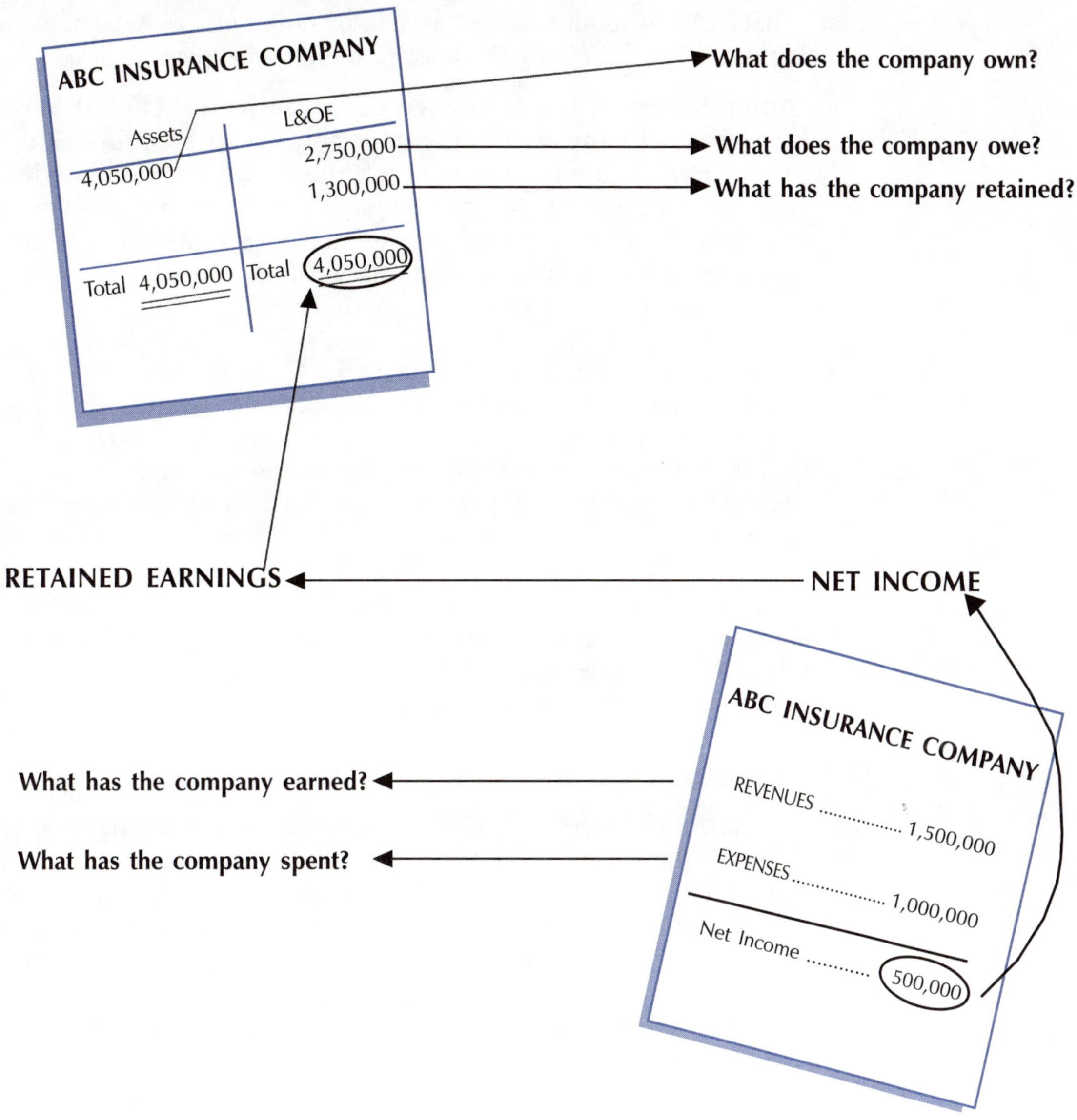

Source: Adapted from Tom Lundin, Jr., *Intro to Insurance Company Accounting* (Atlanta: LOMA © 1999), 4. Used with permission; all rights reserved.

financial statements. The term *generally accepted* means that GAAP is a well-known standard in accounting. Financial statements prepared according to GAAP provide interested users with financial information that is based on common definitions, valuation methods, and formats.

As a result, users of a company's financial information are better able to evaluate the company's financial performance or condition with that of another company or of the same company over time. Without generally accepted standards for reporting financial information, such comparisons would not be meaningful. Note, however, that U.S. GAAP differs in some ways from Canadian GAAP. Throughout this text, we point out these differences where applicable.

- **United States.** A life insurance company in the United States prepares its financial statements according to U.S. GAAP if it or its parent company issues stock that is traded publicly. Mutual and fraternal insurance companies must also comply with U.S. GAAP if they sell debt to raise money or if they offer equity-based insurance products, such as variable annuities, variable life insurance, or universal life insurance.

- **Canada.** Life insurance companies in Canada prepare their financial statements according to Canadian GAAP for both regulators and stockholders. The Canadian ***Annual Return***, which is a document that presents information about an insurer's operations and financial performance, with an emphasis on demonstrating the insurer's solvency and profitability, is also prepared using Canadian GAAP. Thus, insurers in Canada typically comply with only one set of financial reporting requirements—Canadian GAAP. Under specified circumstances, however, the Office of the Superintendent of Financial Institutions may supersede or overrule Canadian GAAP requirements.

Statutory Accounting Practices and Codification—United States

Besides complying with GAAP requirements when applicable, all life insurance companies in the United States must also comply with statutory accounting practices, which support a type of financial accounting that primarily focuses on the requirements of insurance regulators and the interests of policyowners. ***Statutory accounting practices (SAPs)*** are the accounting standards that all life insurers in the United States must follow when preparing the Annual Statement and specified other financial reports that are submitted to regulators. The U.S. ***Annual Statement*** is a document that presents information about an insurer's operations and financial performance, with an emphasis on demonstrating the insurer's solvency.

U.S. GAAP and statutory accounting practices sometimes follow different rules. As a result, insurers in the United States often must prepare two different sets of financial statements: one for U.S. GAAP and another for statutory requirements. Further, statutory requirements often vary by state. To minimize this complication, a process—called ***codification***—was undertaken to help standardize financial reporting requirements among the 50 states. The purpose of codification is to develop one set of comprehensive statutory guidelines.

Individual states still maintain their right to adopt specific accounting rules, although the intended result of the codification of statutory accounting practices is a single, comprehensive document specifying statutory accounting practices. Insurers began preparing the U.S. Annual Statement under codified statutory accounting as of January 2001. Throughout this textbook, we discuss the impact of codification as it applies to an insurer's financial reporting requirements, particularly if it differs from U.S. GAAP.

International Accounting Standards

Most countries develop accounting standards with which companies must comply for financial reporting purposes. Currently, international companies must comply with separate, sometimes conflicting, financial reporting requirements in each country in which they conduct business. The ***International Accounting Standards Committee (IASC)*** is an organization charged with promulgating accounting standards that are applicable internationally, independent of the home country of the company issuing the financial statements. The Securities and Exchange Commission, which we discuss later in this chapter, is charged with monitoring the impact of international accounting standards on financial reporting requirements for companies that conduct business in the United States.

Management Accounting

Management accounting is the process of identifying, measuring, analyzing, and communicating financial information. The primary difference between the two major fields of accounting is that management accounting focuses primarily on planning for future performance, whereas financial accounting focuses on reporting past performance. Reflecting this focus, management accounting includes activities that are designed to analyze operating costs, oversee budgets, and evaluate the profitability of various products and services. However, many of the accounting standards applied to management accounting are the same accounting standards as those used for financial accounting.

Figure 1-3 lists the types of financial reports that are prepared under financial accounting—either GAAP or statutory accounting practices—and management accounting.

The Accounting Function

Either internal employees or external parties can gather and report a company's financial information. The information communicated for management accounting typically is gathered and reported by the

FIGURE 1-3. Financial Reports and the Fields of Accounting.

TYPE OF ACCOUNTING	TYPICAL FINANCIAL REPORTS PREPARED
Financial Accounting (U.S. GAAP and Canadian GAAP)	• Annual Report (U.S.) • Annual Return (Canada) • Annual Report to Stockholders and Policyholders (Canada)
Financial Accounting (U.S. Statutory Accounting Practices)	• Annual Statement (U.S.)
Management Accounting	• Sales Forecasts • Budgets • Detailed Financial Information by Line of Business

Source: Adapted from Tom Lundin, Jr., *Intro to Insurance Company Accounting* (Atlanta: LOMA, © 1999), 9. Used with permission; all rights reserved.

company's internal accounting employees. As shown in Figure 1-4, a company's accounting function includes people and processes that collect and record information for current and future use about the company's business transactions.

An insurance company's accounting system enables the company's management to make sound business decisions, satisfy financial reporting requirements, identify trends and the opportunities and challenges that the company faces, and develop appropriate strategies to take advantage of the opportunities and to reduce or eliminate the challenges. The accounting function is generally split into the fields of public accounting and private accounting.

Public Accounting

The main focus of public accounting is to provide, for the benefit of external parties, an external review of, and an independent opinion on, a company's financial statements. Public accountants are employed by or affiliated with a public accounting company or governmental regulatory authority.

FIGURE 1-4. How an Accounting System Works.

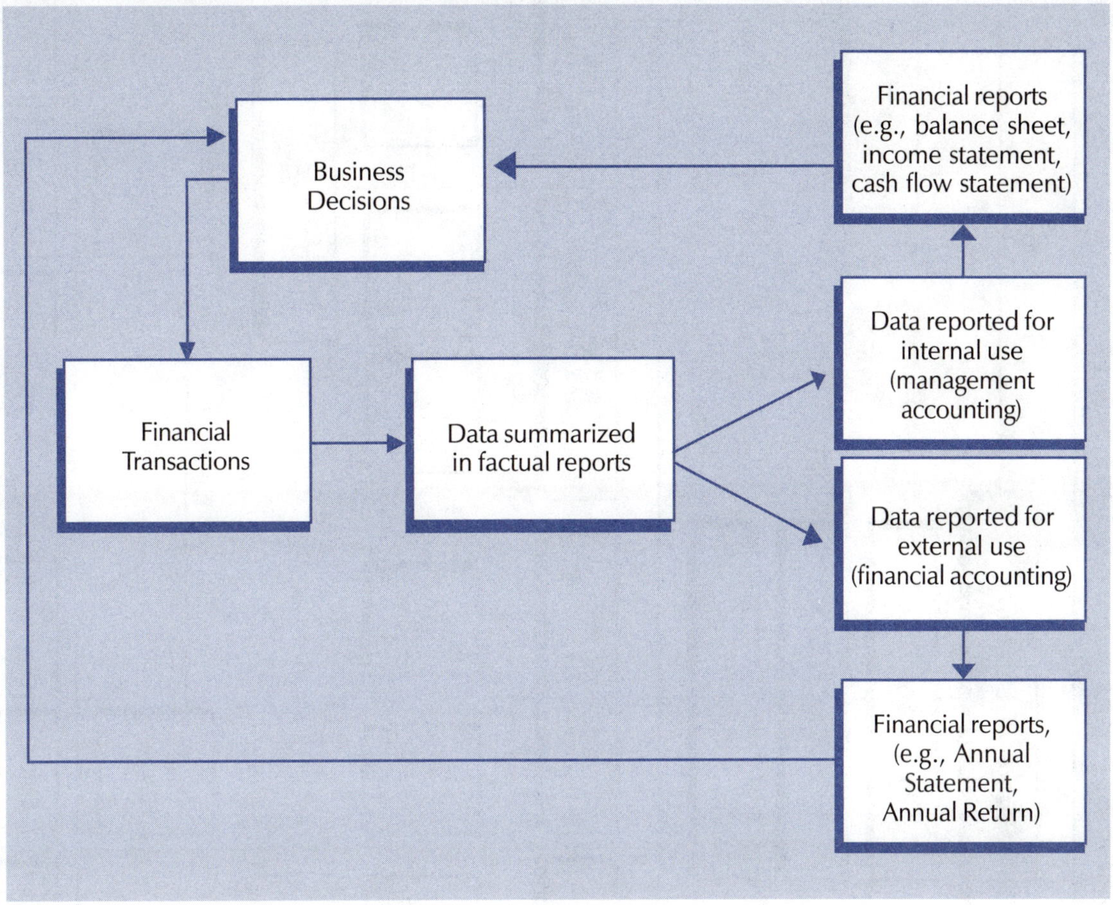

Private Accounting

Accountants who are company employees and who perform the company's accounting function are classified as private accountants. Typically, private accountants prepare financial statements for the company's external parties and management accounting reports for the company's internal users of financial information.

The head of a company's accounting function is typically called the ***controller*** or *comptroller.* Although a controller usually reports to the company's chief financial officer, reporting relationships among the controller and other company officers and employees vary among companies. Figure 1-5 provides an example of one way a life insurance company can organize its accounting function.

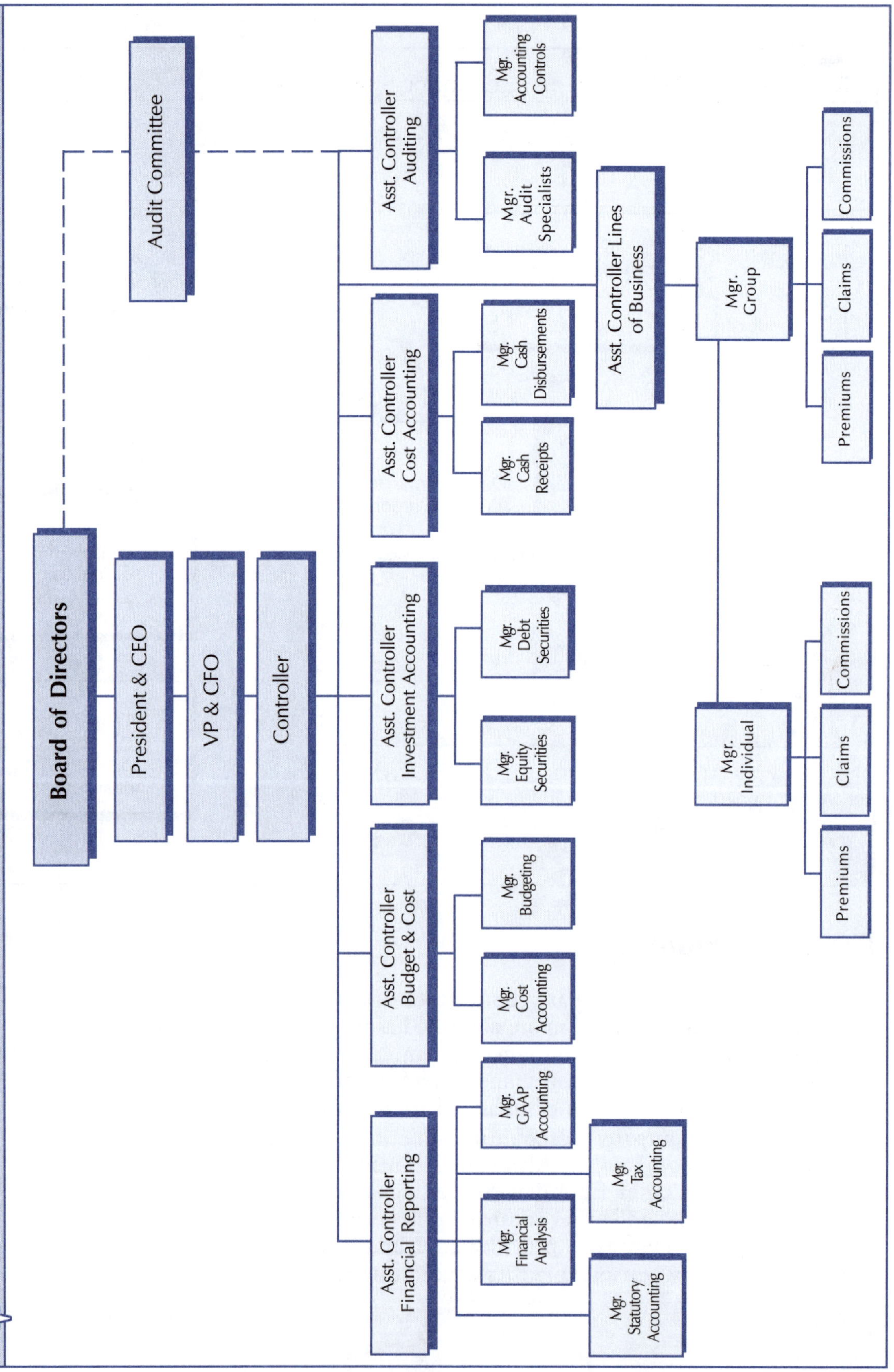

FIGURE 1-5. Organization of the Accounting Function in a Life Insurance Company.

Typical activities that private accountants perform in insurance companies are to

- Develop and maintain adequate internal controls to safeguard the insurer's holdings and to ensure the accuracy of financial statements
- Establish and maintain the insurer's accounting records
- Keep records associated with all financial transactions involving the insurer's receipt or disbursement of money
- Prepare and analyze financial statements and financial reports
- Interpret and analyze operating costs and budgeted amounts

Accounting Regulation in the United States

Because the insurance industry manages large amounts of money, and because many people rely on insurers for financial protection, the public can be injured if insurance companies do not adhere to prudent standards in their business transactions. The financial health of the insurance industry is deemed to be in the public's best interest. Thus, financial reporting requirements help to ensure that each insurer provides adequately for the eventual payment of contractual benefits. To make informed decisions, policyowners, investors, and other interested parties must rely on the information presented in an insurer's financial statements. Several regulatory and private agencies have developed industry guidelines and state laws and regulations that insurers follow to prepare financial statements that are fair, timely, and accurate. Five organizations have a significant impact on accounting and financial reporting for life insurance companies in the United States. The following sections briefly discuss these organizations.

National Association of Insurance Commissioners

The ***National Association of Insurance Commissioners (NAIC)*** is an association of state insurance commissioners designed to promote consistent insurance regulation. Although the NAIC has no legislative power, its recommendations and actions strongly influence the individual state insurance commissioners, the state legislatures, and the insurance industry. The NAIC's influence on insurance accounting is strongest with respect to the U.S. Annual Statement, the completion of which forms the basis of statutory accounting practices in the United States. Each state determines which NAIC recommendations it approves or modifies, then incorporates these recommendations into its state reporting requirements for insurers.

The NAIC specifies the format and content of the Annual Statement. Insurers in the United States must file this document with the NAIC and with the insurance department in every state in which the insurers conduct business. Insurers in Canada, as well as other international insurers who conduct business in the United States, must also comply with statutory reporting requirements for each state in which they conduct business. The NAIC uses information in the Annual Statement to evaluate an insurer's financial condition as well as its compliance with insurance laws and regulatory requirements.

Internal Revenue Service

The Internal Revenue Service (IRS), a part of the U.S. Department of the Treasury, is the governmental agency responsible for enforcing the provisions of laws and regulations concerning income taxes in the United States. Insurers in the United States must adhere to the tax code of the IRS. The IRS significantly influences the way in which insurance companies conduct business. Taxation accounting addresses the reporting and filing requirements related to taxation. A discussion of tax accounting, the tax code, and specific tax effects on an insurer's products is beyond the scope of this text.

American Institute of Certified Public Accountants

The ***American Institute of Certified Public Accountants (AICPA)*** is a professional association of U.S. Certified Public Accountants (CPAs). The AICPA has no regulatory powers, but its influence is widespread. Through its Auditing Standards Board, the AICPA develops generally accepted auditing standards (GAAS), which public accountants use when conducting audits of an insurer's financial statements. The AICPA directly influences accounting practices in several ways: through technical advisory committees, *Statements of Position (SOPs)*, *Technical Bulletins* and other publications, and its code of professional conduct for accounting professionals.

Securities and Exchange Commission

The ***Securities and Exchange Commission (SEC)*** is a federal government agency that regulates the investment industry in the United States. Its main purpose is to protect investors. The SEC has jurisdiction over all public companies—that is, corporations whose stocks or bonds are offered for sale to the public in the United States. The

SEC holds the legal authority to prescribe the accounting methods that public companies use. Many insurers are subject to SEC regulations. The following tests determine whether SEC regulations apply to an insurer operating in the United States:

- **Is an insurer a stock company?** All publicly traded stock companies, including insurers, are subject to SEC regulation.
- **Does the company sell equity-based products, such as variable annuities or variable life insurance?** Equity-based products are subject to SEC regulation because they are investment products as well as insurance products, and the SEC regulates investment products. Under this test, mutual and fraternal insurers that offer equity-based products are subject to SEC regulation, even though they are not publicly traded stock companies.

Insurers that are subject to SEC regulation generally must submit U.S. GAAP-based financial statements to the SEC. Currently, mutual and fraternal insurers that sell equity-based products can submit statutory financial statements to the SEC.

Financial Accounting Standards Board

The SEC has delegated its responsibility for establishing U.S. GAAP to the ***Financial Accounting Standards Board (FASB)***, a private organization funded by the accounting profession and companies with an interest in accounting practices. The primary role of FASB (pronounced *faz-bee*) is to establish and promote the use of GAAP. FASB pronouncements, which apply to insurance companies that conduct business in the United States, identify the standards for financial reporting.

Companies must report all significant departures from FASB pronouncements, which are typically referred to as *Statements of Financial Accounting Standards (SFAS)*. Because of the potential confusion that could result from the numerous publications and pronouncements that focus on GAAP, the AICPA established a GAAP hierarchy. Figure 1-6 describes the hierarchy for statutory accounting practices as a result of codification. Note that the GAAP hierarchy, which describes the order of authority of sources of GAAP information, is included in the statutory accounting practices hierarchy.

Accounting Regulation in Canada

Both federal and provincial organizations influence insurance accounting in Canada. Key organizations that influence insurance

FIGURE 1-6. The Statutory Accounting Practices Hierarchy.

The following hierarchy is not intended to preempt state legislative and regulatory authority.

LEVEL 1

- SSAPs (statements of statutory accounting practices) including GAAP reference material Categories a, b and c from the GAAP Hierarchy, as defined in *Statement of Auditing Standards No. 69, The Meaning of Present Fairly in Conformity with GAAP* (SAS 69), to the extent it has been adopted by the NAIC and in the order of hierarchy specified by the AICPA.
- Category a includes: FASB Statements and Interpretations, APB Opinions, and AICPA Accounting Research Bulletins.
- Category b includes: FASB Technical Bulletins, AICPA Industry Audit and Accounting Guides, and AICPA Statements of Position.
- Category c includes: Consensus positions of the FASB Emerging Issues Task Force and AICPA Practice Bulletins.

LEVEL 2

- Consensus positions of the Emerging Accounting Issues Working Group as adopted by the NAIC

LEVEL 3

- NAIC Annual Statement Instructions
- NAIC *Purposes and Procedures of the Securities Valuation Office* manual

LEVEL 4

- Statutory Accounting Principles Statement of Concepts

LEVEL 5

- GAAP reference material under Category c in the GAAP Hierarchy

Source: Excerpted from NAIC, *Accounting Practices and Procedures Manual: Effective January 1, 2001 as of March 2000*, v. 1 (Kansas City, MO: NAIC, 1999, 2000), P-8. Reprinted with permission from the National Association of Insurance Commissioners.

accounting in Canada include the Office of the Superintendent of Financial Institutions, the Canada Customs and Revenue Agency, and the Canadian Institute of Chartered Accountants, which we describe in the following sections.

Office of the Superintendent of Financial Institutions

The agency primarily responsible for overseeing federally registered insurance companies in Canada and ensuring their compliance with federal laws and regulations is the ***Office of the Superintendent of Financial Institutions (OSFI)***. OSFI issues the Canadian Annual Return, which is similar to the U.S. Annual Statement. OSFI also establishes financial reporting requirements for insurers in Canada and international insurers that conduct business in Canada. In addition, OSFI monitors the financial stability of provincially registered insurance companies that have policyholders in more than one province.

Provincially registered life insurance companies are subject to the Civil Code in the province of Quebec and common law in the remaining Canadian provinces. Specifically, life insurance companies that are registered only in Quebec must comply with the requirements of the Inspecteur Général des Institutions Financières (IGIF), which is similar in scope and responsibility to OSFI. Provincially registered life insurers in Quebec submit an annual report, called the Q91 report, to IGIF. They may also submit a copy of the Q91 to OSFI, although they are not obligated to do so.

Canada Customs and Revenue Agency

The ***Canada Customs and Revenue Agency***, formerly called *Revenue Canada*, is the governmental agency responsible for enforcing the provisions of Canadian laws and regulations concerning income taxes. The function of the Canada Customs and Revenue Agency is similar to that of the IRS in the United States.

Canadian Institute of Chartered Accountants

The ***Canadian Institute of Chartered Accountants (CICA)*** establishes Canadian GAAP for insurers to follow in recording and presenting their financial information. The CICA develops GAAP pronouncements for insurance companies that operate in Canada. The CICA contributes to governmental legislative deliberations in the areas of accounting and finance. In addition, the CICA has a consultative relationship with the Canada Customs and Revenue Agency and several other related agencies at both the federal and provincial levels. The CICA establishes national auditing and accounting standards for financial reporting.

Course Overview

This course provides an overview of the concepts of financial accounting, management accounting, and financial reporting requirements for life insurance companies in the United States and Canada. The course is divided into two texts: (1) *The Accounting Function and Management Accounting in Life Insurance Companies* and (2) *Financial Accounting and Reporting Requirements in Life Insurance Companies*. The first text discusses the accounting function, accounting concepts and principles, and management accounting. The second text discusses accounting for typical insurance company transactions, financial reporting requirements, and financial ratio analysis for life insurance companies in the United States and Canada. The CD-ROM that accompanies the second text includes examples of insurance company financial statements, which will enable you to apply some of the key concepts you will learn in this course.

Key Terms and Concepts

accounting
financial transaction
solvency
profitability
financial accounting
financial statements
balance sheet
income statement
cash flow statement
statement of owners' equity
generally accepted accounting principles (GAAP)
Annual Return
statutory accounting practices (SAPs)
Annual Statement
codification
International Accounting Standards Committee (IASC)
management accounting
controller
National Association of Insurance Commissioners (NAIC)
Internal Revenue Service (IRS)
American Institute of Certified Public Accountants (AICPA)
Securities and Exchange Commission (SEC)
Financial Accounting Standards Board (FASB)
Office of the Superintendent of Financial Institutions (OSFI)
Canada Customs and Revenue Agency
Canadian Institute of Chartered Accountants (CICA)

Chapter 2

The Accounting Cycle

Chapter Outline

Objectives

After reading this chapter, you should be able to

- Identify the major account classifications that appear on an insurer's balance sheet and income statement
- Identify the basic accounting equation and recognize its relationship to the account classifications on the balance sheet and the income statement
- Describe an insurer's operating cycle and identify the primary sources and uses of an insurer's funds
- Recognize the difference between temporary accounts and permanent accounts and normal balances of debit or credit in an account

Chapter 1 introduced the subject of accounting and the key players in a life insurer's accounting function. Chapter 2 introduces you to account classification, the basic accounting equation, an insurer's operating cycle, and double-entry accounting.

Account Classification

The business transactions that a company records in its accounting system and reports on its financial statements typically involve five basic account classifications: (1) assets, (2) liabilities, (3) owners' equity, (4) revenues, and (5) expenses. These account classifications comprise a company's ***chart of accounts***, which is a numbered or alphabetical list of all the company's account names. An ***account*** is the basic tool that a company uses to record, group, and summarize similar types of business transactions. Figure 2-1 shows a typical chart of accounts.

Each insurer devises its own chart of accounts. Developing and maintaining a company's chart of accounts is typically the responsibility of the company's controller. Account titles and numbering schemes vary from insurer to insurer because each insurer has a unique chart of

FIGURE 2-1. A Typical Chart of Accounts.

The account divisions on a typical chart of accounts answer the five basic business questions:

1001. Assets	What does the company own?
2001. Liabilities	What does the company owe?
4001. Owners' Equity	What does the company retain?
7001. Revenue	What does the company earn?
8001. Expenses	What does the company spend?

Source: Adapted from Tom Lundin, Jr., *Intro to Insurance Company Accounting* (Atlanta: LOMA, © 1999), 18. Used with permission; all rights reserved.

accounts. In this text, we will use simple, descriptive account titles in our examples, so you can clearly see the effect that business transactions have on an insurer's financial condition and performance.

Assets: What Does the Insurer Own?

Assets, the first account classification on the balance sheet, are all items, generally of readily determinable monetary value, that a company owns. Assets can be tangible (physical), like buildings and computer equipment, or intangible (not physical), such as stocks, bonds, and other investments. Items that are receivable—that is, contractual promises of payment by another party to the company—are also assets. Assets represent a company's resources for generating cash, which the company can use to fulfill its financial obligations. For example, insurance companies typically invest in bonds, an asset. Whenever the bonds pay interest, mature, or are sold by an insurer, the insurer receives cash, which it can use to settle policyowner claims or other financial commitments.

Under GAAP, insurers list their assets on a balance sheet in order of ***liquidity***, which is the ease with which an asset can be converted to cash with little or no loss in value. On a GAAP-based balance sheet, an insurer's most liquid assets would be listed first, followed by other short-term assets, and then long-term assets. ***Short-term assets*** are assets that a company expects to readily convert into cash or consume within the current accounting period, typically one year. Cash and cash equivalents—such as certificates of deposit (CDs)—are examples of short-term assets. An insurer's premiums due and receivable is another example of a short-term asset, because the insurer expects to receive premium payments for insurance coverage within the year.

Long-term assets are assets that a company plans to hold indefinitely or for a long time—in other words, more than a year—to generate income. Compared with short-term assets, long-term assets usually take longer to convert to cash. Real estate and property and equipment are examples of an insurer's long-term assets. Figure 2-2 depicts the assets section of an insurer's GAAP-based balance sheet.

Note that, under statutory accounting practices, insurers in the United States typically list their investments first, followed by cash and cash equivalents, and then other assets. In other words, assets are not listed solely in order of liquidity on a statutory balance sheet.

Liabilities: What Does the Insurer Owe?

Liabilities, which comprise the second major account classification on the balance sheet, are a company's monetary values for its current

FIGURE 2-2. Assets Portion of the Balance Sheet.

ABC Life Insurance Company
Balance Sheet
($000s)
as of December 31, 2001

Assets	
Investments:	
Debt securities	13,182,326
Equity securities	620,026
Mortgages and real estate	1,136,750
Other long-term investments	201,726
Short-term investments	566,689
Total Investments	15,707,517
Cash and cash equivalents	223,413
Premiums receivable	331,977
Property and equipment	461,246
Other assets	328,823
Total Assets	17,052,976

and future obligations. Liabilities result from a monetary commitment that the company's management has made on behalf of the company. As such, liabilities represent demands against the company's assets. An amount that is payable—that is, an amount that the company has promised to pay to another party—is a liability.

In order to remain in business, an insurer must have a higher monetary value for its assets than for its liabilities. Most liabilities consist of the actual and expected commitments to, and claims of, its policyowners, annuitants, and beneficiaries. Insurance companies typically list their liabilities on the balance sheet according to their financial impact—in descending order, from largest to smallest dollar amount—on the company. Therefore, liabilities for future contractual benefits, which represent the largest monetary amount of an insurer's liabilities, are listed first.

Obligations that must be paid in one year or less are called ***short-term liabilities***. Liabilities that do not have be paid in full during the current accounting period—usually one year—are called ***long-term liabilities***. Keep in mind that short-term and long-term liabilities are a GAAP concept. For statutory reporting purposes, an insurer would list its contractual reserves first, followed by other reserves, and then other liabilities. Figure 2-3 depicts the liabilities section of the GAAP-based balance sheet of a life insurance company.

Owners' Equity: What Has the Insurer Retained?

Owners' equity, the third major account classification on the balance sheet, represents the owners' investment in the company. The components of owners' equity represent a residual claim against a company's assets. In other words, if a company goes out of business, in theory, the company's owners—that is, the stockholders of a stock insurer or the policyowners of a mutual or fraternal insurer—are entitled to whatever remains of the company's assets after all creditor and policyowner claims have been paid. In this sense, owners' equity

FIGURE 2-3. Liabilities Portion of the Balance Sheet.

ABC Life Insurance Company
Balance Sheet
($000s)
as of December 31, 2001

Liabilities	
Future contractual benefits:	
Life insurance	7,032,225
Annuities	3,627,905
Accident and health	2,780,114
Advance premiums	402,846
Unpaid policy claims	812,066
Total Contractual Liabilities	14,655,156
Notes payable	222,062
Commissions payable	918,133
Total Liabilities	15,795,351

is the difference between a company's assets and its liabilities, as follows:

Owners' equity = Assets – Liabilities

For specified purposes, insurance companies replace the term *owners' equity* with *capital and surplus*. ***Capital*** represents the money that an insurer's owners have invested in the insurer. ***Surplus*** is the cumulative monetary amount, under statutory accounting practices, that remains in the insurance company over time. An insurer's surplus for a particular reporting period is calculated as the insurer's assets minus its liabilities and capital for that period. Keep in mind that sometimes the term *capital* by itself is used to refer to an insurer's owners' equity. Generally, we can also say that, for insurers:

Capital [+ Surplus] = Assets – Liabilities

Because mutual and fraternal insurers do not have stockholders, their capital and surplus accounts typically consist entirely of surplus. In other words, a mutual or fraternal insurer's capital equals zero. Thus, we can say that, for mutual and fraternal insurers:

Surplus = Assets – Liabilities

Another owners' equity account is retained earnings. ***Retained earnings*** is a GAAP account that represents the cumulative amount of a company's earnings that has been kept in the company over time to finance the company's ongoing operations. The *Retained Earnings* account is not used in statutory accounting. For statutory reporting purposes, an insurer uses the *Surplus* account to report the cumulative amount of its earnings over time. Note, however, that the monetary amounts in an insurer's *Retained Earnings* account under GAAP and *Surplus* account under statutory accounting may differ because of different formulas for calculating surplus under statutory accounting.

Figure 2-4 depicts a portion of the owners' equity section of a stock insurer's balance sheet. Next, we discuss account classification on the insurer's income statement.

Revenues: What Has the Insurer Earned?

Revenues, the first group of accounts on the income statement, represent the amounts earned from a company's core business

FIGURE 2-4. Owners' Equity Portion of the Balance Sheet.

ABC Life Insurance Company
Balance Sheet
($000s)
as of December 31, 2001

Owners' Equity	
Common stock of $10 par value.	
Authorized and issued 8,500 shares	85,000
Additional paid-in capital	40,000
Retained earnings	1,144,625
Treasury stock	(12,000)
Total Owners' Equity	1,257,625

operations. For insurance companies, core business operations include the sale of products and services to customers, investment income, and fee income from providing administrative or management services.

Insurers receive investment income from investments that they own. Keep in mind that the investments that an insurer owns are assets, but the earnings on these assets are classified generally as revenues and specifically as investment income. Thus, insurers report their investments on the balance sheet and their earnings on those investments on the income statement. Fee income typically is generated from providing management services or administrative services to the insurer's customers.

An increase in revenues typically increases assets. For example, when a policyowner pays a policy premium, this transaction increases not only an insurer's revenues, but also its cash, which is an asset account. Figure 2-5 depicts the revenues section of an insurer's income statement.

Expenses: What Has the Insurer Spent?

Expenses, the second major account classification on the income statement, represent the amount of one or more assets that a company

FIGURE 2-5. Revenues Portion of the Income Statement.

ABC Life Insurance Company Income Statement ($000s) for the year ended December 31, 2001	
Revenues	
Premium income	5,123,674
Net investment income	799,723
Fee income	80,255
Total Revenues	6,003,652

uses to receive a certain benefit or service. Expenses are a necessary part of doing business, because a company cannot generate revenues without also incurring expenses. Investment expenses and general and administrative expenses are typical expenses that insurance companies incur in the course of conducting business.

Investment expenses are the costs that an insurer incurs from buying, holding, and selling investments such as bonds and real estate. General and administrative expenses include (1) contractual benefit expenses and (2) operating expenses. Contractual benefit expenses, which are unique to insurance companies, include payments for annuity withdrawals, cash surrenders, and life insurance claims. Operating expenses include agent commissions, advertising costs, salaries of home office employees, rent and utilities on the home office building, and home office supplies used to indirectly support the generation of revenues.

Unlike revenues, expenses decrease a company's assets. For example, when an insurer pays a policy claim (an expense), the insurer's cash (an asset) decreases. Figure 2-6 depicts the expenses portion of an income statement.

For each accounting period, the insurer prepares an income statement to determine its net income or net loss for the period. ***Net income*** is an excess of total revenues over total expenses. Likewise, a ***net loss*** is an excess of total expenses over total revenues. Losses, which are negative amounts, are presented on financial statements

FIGURE 2-6. Expenses Portion of the Income Statement.

ABC Life Insurance Company
Income Statement
($000s)
for the year ended December 31, 2001

Expenses	
Contractual benefits	4,332,003
Operating expenses:	
Agent commissions	651,786
Insurance expenses	558,813
Other operating expenses	101,547
Total Operating Expenses	1,312,146
Total Benefits and Expenses	5,644,149

in parentheses. Generally, the income statement separates gains—increases in revenue—and losses—decreases in revenue—derived from a company's core business operations from gains and losses derived from transactions outside the company's normal business operations. One example of a core business operation in a life insurance company is the sale of products and services to the company's individual and group policyowners. Figure 2-7 summarizes the steps to calculate an insurer's net income or net loss.

To compute its net gain (net loss) from operations, an insurer first subtracts the expenses it incurred from normal business operations from the revenues earned from those operations. A ***net gain from operations*** results if a company's operating revenues exceed its operating expenses. Conversely, if the company's operating expenses exceed its operating revenues, then the result is a ***net loss from operations***. The insurer then subtracts policyowner dividends and federal income taxes, and adds gains (losses) from transactions outside its core business operations from its net gain (loss) from operations to determine the net income or net loss for the period.

FIGURE 2-7. Calculation of Net Income.

	Total Revenues
–	Total Expenses
=	Net Gain (Loss) from Operations
–	Dividends to Policyowners
–	Federal Income Taxes
+	Realized Gains (Losses)
=	Net Income (Loss)

Source: Adapted from Tom Lundin, Jr., *Intro to Insurance Company Accounting* (Atlanta: LOMA, © 1999), 109. Used with permission; all rights reserved.

The Basic Accounting Equation

The basic accounting equation is fundamental to the accounting function. The ***basic accounting equation***, sometimes called the *balance sheet equation*, is a mathematical depiction of the relationship among the three key account classifications—assets, liabilities, and owners' equity—on the balance sheet. This relationship is expressed in the following equation:

Assets = Liabilities + Owners' Equity

Recall that, for insurance companies, we can substitute Capital and Surplus for Owners' Equity, as follows:

Assets = Liabilities + Capital + Surplus

The balance in the Capital accounts of mutual insurance companies is statistically insignificant. Therefore, *Surplus* is the key

Owners' Equity account for mutual insurers. We can simplify the basic accounting equation for mutual insurers as follows:

Assets = Liabilities + Surplus

Recall that asset, liability, and owners' equity accounts appear on an insurer's balance sheet and that revenue and expense accounts appear on the insurer's income statement. Because revenues and expenses are ultimately closed out at the end of an accounting period to owners' equity, we can expand the basic accounting equation to include all five key account classifications:

Assets = Liabilities + Owners' Equity + Revenues – Expenses

The Operating Cycle

Insurance companies are part of the financial services industry, which is made up of financial institutions that help consumers and businesses save, borrow, invest, and manage money. Each financial institution has a distinctive operating cycle. The interrelationship among financial institutions depends in part on the operating cycle of each institution. The ***operating cycle*** is the way in which funds flow through a company as it conducts its day-to-day business activities. Tracking the flow of funds through a company is a primary focus of the accounting function, which records and reports the transactions associated with an insurer's operating cycle. Figure 2-8 depicts an insurer's typical operating cycle.

Sources of Funds

In accounting terminology, funds flowing into a company are a source of funds and funds flowing out of the company are a use of funds. Typical sources of an insurer's funds are the revenues generated from the insurer's core business activities: (1) premium income, (2) investment income, and (3) fee income. In exchange for accepting the responsibility for managing specified insurance risks, the insurer earns income. When an insurer agrees to accept financial risk, the insurer issues an insurance policy. An insurance policy is a legal contract that obligates the insurer to pay contractual benefits—usually a specified amount of money—when or if a specified loss

FIGURE 2-8. A Typical Operating Cycle.

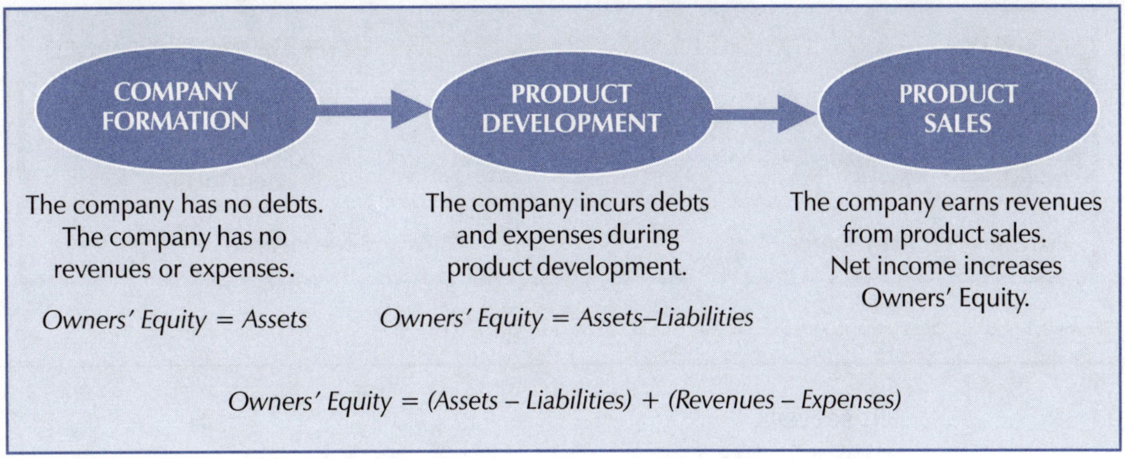

Source: Adapted from Tom Lundin, Jr., *Intro to Insurance Company Accounting* (Atlanta: LOMA, © 1999), 5. Used with permission; all rights reserved.

occurs. The income that the insurer receives for assuming the financial risk associated with this specified loss is called ***premium income***.

As an insurer receives premium income, the income is invested and more income is earned on these investments. The amount of investment income that an insurer receives from its investing activities affects other elements of its operating cycle. Besides generating premium income and investment income from their core business operations, insurance companies also earn other income, primarily in the form of fees. Fee income is a small, but growing, source of funds for some life insurance companies. Insurers typically obtain fee income by providing brokerage services, management services for separate (segregated) accounts, and third-party administration services performed for other insurers. In sum, an insurer's sources of funds represent revenues and answer the question: What has the insurer earned? Figure 2-9 summarizes these three sources of funds.

Uses of Funds

An insurance company's primary uses of funds are paying its obligations on time and paying the expenses the company incurs to support its income-generating activities. Typical uses of funds for insurance companies include establishing reserves for future contractual benefits and paying current contractual benefits, agent commissions, and taxes.

FIGURE 2-9. Insurers' Sources of Funds.

ACTIVITY	TYPE OF INCOME EARNED
Product sales of life insurance policies and annuity contracts	**Premium income**
Investment in assets	**Investment income**
Providing services for fees	**Fee income**

Source: Adapted from Tom Lundin, Jr., *Intro to Insurance Company Accounting* (Atlanta: LOMA, © 1999), 46. Used with permission; all rights reserved.

Reserves

Insurers hold their policyowners' funds in trust until contractual benefit payments are paid in full or until the policy or contract lapses, expires, or is cancelled. For this reason, insurance companies have a fiduciary (trust) relationship with their policyowners. To meet its fiduciary obligations, an insurer must set aside the funds necessary to meet those obligations as they become due. ***Reserves,*** called *actuarial liabilities* on Canadian financial statements, are liability accounts that identify the amounts of money that an insurer expects to need to meet its future business obligations. An insurer's reserves comprise the largest portion of its total liabilities.

Contractual Benefits

Because insurance companies earn most of their revenues from the sale of insurance policies and annuity contracts, one of an insurer's main uses of funds is to pay contractual benefits. Contractual benefits are requests from policyowners and beneficiaries for payments of amounts that are due. Such benefit payments, which are the largest use of funds, account for more than half the total cash outflows of insurers in the United States and Canada.

Policy Dividends

Insurers also use funds to pay policy dividends, usually on life insurance policies, although insurers may also pay policy dividends to owners of participating annuity contracts. A ***policy dividend*** is a portion of an insurer's surplus that is paid to the policyowner of a participating policy. A participating policy gives the policyowner the right to share in the insurer's surplus. Policy dividends are paid when the insurer's mortality (death rate) experience is more favorable than its expected experience. In essence, a policy dividend is a return of premium to the policyowner. Policy dividends should not be confused with stockholder dividends, which are payments to the owners of stock insurance companies.

Agent Commissions and Salaries

Agent commissions and salaries are a large use of an insurer's funds. Most individual life insurance policies are sold on a commission basis, although group life insurance products are typically sold through a salaried agent system.

Operating Expenses

All companies pay various ***operating expenses***, which are the expenses that a company incurs in conducting its normal business operations. An insurer's operating expenses are similar to those of many noninsurance companies, and include such items as rent, maintenance, advertising, travel, and legal expenses.

Taxes, Licenses, and Fees

Life insurers pay many of the same kinds of taxes that many noninsurance companies pay, including property taxes and unemployment taxes. In addition, insurers pay some insurance-specific taxes and fees, such as premium taxes and licensing fees.

Figure 2-10 summarizes an insurer's primary uses of funds and the specific accounts that are typically affected by the activities associated with the insurer's use of funds. Note that *Cash*, an asset account, is also affected, because the insurer's cash is decreased when amounts are paid out.

Double-Entry Accounting

The accounting function tracks and reports an insurer's transactions through the use of double-entry accounting. Under ***double-entry accounting***,

- Every financial transaction has at least one debit and one credit
- The total monetary amount of the debits must equal that of the credits for each transaction
- Each accounting entry must maintain the balance of the basic accounting equation

FIGURE 2-10. Insurers' Uses of Funds.

Activity	Accounts Affected by Activity
Establishment of liabilities for future fiduciary obligations	Contractual reserves, Claim reserves (liabilities)
Payment of benefits for in-force contracts	Contractual benefit expenses (expense) Cash (asset)
Payment of policy dividends to participating life insurance policyowners	Policy dividends (retained earnings—GAAP; surplus—statutory accounting practices Cash (asset)
Payment of agent commissions and salaries	Agent commissions, Agent salaries (expense) Cash (asset)
Payment of operating expenses	Operating expenses (expense) Cash (asset)
Payment of taxes, licenses, fees	Taxes, licenses, and fees (expense) Cash (asset)

We discuss accounting entries and the basic accounting equation in the following sections.

Accounting Entries

An ***accounting entry***, also called a *journal entry*, is a record of a financial transaction. Each accounting entry includes at least one debit and one credit that show the monetary amount of the transaction. In order for an activity to be considered a business transaction, the activity must have a financial impact on the company—that is, the company must be able to assign an objective monetary value to the transaction.

A company obtains information on the monetary value of a business transaction from source documents. ***Source documents*** are the various business papers and electronic forms that contain original information about a company's business transactions. Source documents verify that a business transaction occurred, as well as the details of the transaction, such as the date, monetary amount, and who approved the transaction. Figure 2-11 lists some typical source documents for insurance companies.

FIGURE 2-11. Source Documents for Financial Transactions.

- ☑ Approved policy applications
- ☑ Premium notices
- ☑ Policy surrender forms
- ☑ Claim forms
- ☑ Checks
- ☑ Receipts

- ☑ Invoices
- ☑ Purchase orders
- ☑ Employee time sheets or time cards
- ☑ Confirmations of investment purchases and sales

Simple Accounting Entries

A ***simple accounting entry*** is a record of a financial transaction that affects only two accounts, and thus has only one debit and one credit. The accounting entry for the receipt of an annual premium is an example of a transaction that affects only two accounts. Suppose the Longevity Life Insurance Company receives a $2,000 annual premium on a life insurance policy. In this example, only two accounts—*Cash* and *Premium Income*—are affected by this business transaction, as shown below:

	Debit	Credit
Cash	2,000	
Premium Income		2,000
To record the receipt of a $2,000 annual premium.		

All accounting principles and accounting systems follow the dual concept. The ***dual concept*** states that every business transaction has two aspects—called debits and credits—that always equal each other. In an accounting entry, a ***debit*** is a specified change that increases the monetary value of asset accounts and expense accounts, or decreases the monetary value of liability accounts, owners' equity accounts and revenue accounts. In an accounting entry, a ***credit*** is a specified change that increases the monetary value of liability account, owners' equity accounts, and revenue accounts, or decreases the monetary value of asset accounts or expense accounts. In recording a business transaction, debits are usually listed first, followed by credits. In the example above, the debit is to *Cash* and the credit is to *Premium Income*. Note that debits are listed first and to the left and that credits are listed next and offset (indented) to the right.

Compound Accounting Entries

Many business transactions affect more than two accounts. A ***compound accounting entry*** is a record of a financial transaction that affects more than two accounts. Suppose Longevity paid a claim of $10,000 plus interest of $100 to the beneficiary of a life insurance policy. In this example, three accounts—*Death Claims, Interest Expense* and *Cash*—are affected, as shown below:

	Debit	Credit
Death Claims	10,000	
Interest Expense	100	
Cash		10,100

To record the payment of a $10,000 death claim plus $100 interest.

Permanent Accounts and Temporary Accounts

Accounts are either permanent or temporary. A ***permanent account*** is a balance sheet account that has a monetary balance at the beginning of each accounting period. Permanent accounts include *Assets, Liabilities,* and *Owners' Equity*. In contrast, at the end of each accounting period, each ***temporary account***, also called a *nominal account*, is zeroed out to a permanent account on the balance sheet. For this reason, at the beginning of each accounting period, all temporary accounts have a zero balance. Temporary accounts comprise the account classifications included on the income statement: *Revenues* and *Expenses*. Most temporary accounts are closed out to an owners' equity account, such as *Retained Earnings* (GAAP) or *Surplus* (statutory accounting).

Closing Entries

Companies use closing entries to move the balances in their temporary accounts to permanent accounts at the end of the accounting period. A ***closing entry*** is an accounting entry that a company makes at the end of each accounting period to start the next accounting period with a zero balance in its temporary accounts. Revenues and expenses must be closed out at the end of each accounting period. An expense incurred or a revenue earned in one period pertains only to that period, so it cannot also be an expense or a revenue in another period. Let's look at a simplified example.

Suppose an insurer has only two accounts on its income statement: (1) *Revenues* and (2) *Expenses*. Because these are temporary accounts, the balance for each account at the beginning of the accounting period is $0. Therefore, all amounts recorded in these accounts apply to the current period only. On three separate dates, the insurer incurs expenses of $2,000, $100, and $500 for a total of $2,600 in expenses. The insurer also earns revenues on four separate dates in the following amounts: $1,000, $800, $500, and $900. The total in the insurer's *Revenues* account is $3,200.

At the end of the accounting period, the insurer zeroes out *Expenses* for $2,600 and *Revenues* for $3,200. The difference between Revenues and Expenses is $600, which, for the purposes of this example, we assume is the insurer's net income for the accounting period. The insurer in turn adds the $600 in net income to its *Retained Earnings* (GAAP) or *Surplus* (statutory accounting practices) account on the balance sheet. If the insurer had a net loss for the period, the insurer would subtract the loss from either *Retained Earnings* or *Surplus*. After these steps, the insurer's operating cycle begins anew with the next accounting period.

Adjusting Entries

An ***adjusting entry*** is an accounting entry to record internal transactions or correct errors that occur in one or more accounting periods. One example of a transaction that requires an adjusting entry is an advance payment of a policy premium by a policyowner. Generally, an insurer records adjusting entries to account for expenses incurred but not yet paid, revenues earned but not yet received, and changes in reserve accounts. After making the appropriate adjusting entries at the end of each annual accounting period, a company prepares its financial statements, then records the applicable closing entries to ready its accounting records for the start of the next accounting period.

Although adjusting entries typically apply to internal activities, source documents are still required to support these entries. For example, salaries that have been earned by an insurance company's employees during this year, but which the company will not pay until next year, may not yet have a time sheet or the equivalent source document available. Nonetheless, at the end of the accounting period, the company will prepare a source document that shows the amount of the adjusting entry, along with supporting documentation containing details about how the monetary amounts were calculated. Using the general format of debiting an accural account—representing amounts owed for employee salaries, which the insurer has not yet paid—and crediting the payable account, the adjusting entry is as follows:

Accrued Salaries xxx
    Salaries Payable xxx
To adjust for salaries that have been earned but not yet paid.

Next year, upon paying the accrued salaries, the company would debit *Salaries Payable* and credit *Cash* to record this transaction, as follows:

Salaries Payable xxx
    Cash xxx
To pay salaries that were accrued in the previous year.

Normal Account Balances

An account's balance is the monetary amount in the account as of a specified date. To obtain the balance in an account, you would calculate the difference between the account's debits and its credits. When an account's debits exceed its credits, the account is said to have a normal balance of debit. Similarly, when an account's credits exceed its debits, the account is said to have a normal balance of credit. An account's ***normal balance*** is found by determining whether the account's balance is increased by a debit or a credit to the account. Some accounts have a normal balance of debit; other accounts have a normal balance of credit. Accounts that are increased by debits typically have a normal balance of a debit at the end of the accounting period. Accounts that are increased by credits usually have a normal balance of a credit at the end of the accounting period.

Balance Sheet Accounts

Let's look at balance sheet accounts—assets, liabilities, and owners' equity—with respect to the normal balances in these accounts. *Assets* typically have a normal balance of a debit because increases are recorded as debits to asset accounts. Both *Liabilities* and *Owners' Equity* accounts generally have a normal balance of a credit because increases are recorded as credits to these accounts.

Income Statement Accounts

Income statement accounts—*Revenues* and *Expenses*—also have either a normal balance of a debit or a normal balance of a credit. Credits increase *Revenues*, so revenue accounts generally have a normal balance of a credit. Debits increase *Expenses*, so expense accounts typically have a normal balance of a debit.

Figure 2-12 summarizes the normal account balances for these five key account classifications.

FIGURE 2-12. Account Classification: Normal Balances.

DEBITS INCREASE	CREDITS INCREASE
Assets	Liabilities
Expenses	Owners' Equity
	Revenues

Key Terms and Concepts

chart of accounts
account
assets
liquidity
short-term assets
long-term assets
liabilities
short-term liabilities
long-term liabilities
owners' equity
capital
surplus
retained earnings
revenues
expenses
net income
net loss
net gain from operations
net loss from operations
basic accounting equation
operating cycle
premium income
reserves
policy dividend
operating expenses
double-entry accounting
accounting entry
source documents
simple accounting entry
dual concept
debit
credit
compound accounting entry
permanent account
temporary account
closing entry
adjusting entry
normal balance

Chapter 3

Accounting Concepts and Principles

Chapter Outline

Financial Statement Concepts
- Entity Concept
- Going-Concern Concept

Accounting Information Qualities
- Reliability
- Relevance
- Consistency
- Comparability
- Materiality
- Conservatism

Accounting Principles
- Cost Concept
- Measuring-Unit Concept
- Full-Disclosure Concept
- Time-Period Concept
- Revenue Recognition: The Realization Principle
- Expense Recognition: The Matching Principle

Accounting Bases
- Accrual-Basis Accounting
- Cash-Basis Accounting

Objectives

After reading this chapter, you should be able to

- Recognize the two key financial statement concepts—the entity concept and the going-concern concept
- Identify key qualities and characteristics of useable accounting information
- Demonstrate understanding of the accounting principles that guide the recording and reporting of accounting information
- Describe the realization principle and the matching principle in accrual-basis accounting
- Distinguish the difference between accrual-basis accounting and cash-basis accounting

Recall that the primary purpose of the accounting function is to provide information about a company's financial performance. This information is usually contained in the company's financial statements. The information contained in a company's financial statements represents a company's past performance and current financial condition. However, the real value of this information lies in its predictive quality. Accounting information has ***predictive quality*** if it enables interested users to form a reasonably accurate estimate of a company's financial strength or earnings potential.

To ensure that its financial statements have predictive quality, a company follows specified guidelines concerning the

- Type of accounting information that is recorded and reported
- Timing of recording and reporting accounting information
- Processes related to the recording and reporting of accounting information

The application of financial accounting concepts and principles enables companies to address these accounting concerns. Figure 3-1 summarizes the key financial accounting concepts and principles that companies use to record and report accounting information. The following sections discuss these key concepts and principles.

FIGURE 3-1. Key Financial Accounting Concepts and Principles.

Financial Statement Concepts		
Entity concept		Going-concern concept
Accounting Information Qualities		
Reliability	Relevance	Consistency
Comparability	Materiality	Conservatism
Account Maintenance Principles		
Cost concept		Measuring-unit concept
Full-disclosure concept		Time period concept
Accounting Bases		
Accrual-basis accounting		Cash-basis accounting

Financial Statement Concepts

In accounting, the entity concept and the going-concern concept underlie all financial statements. The following sections discuss these two financial statement concepts.

Entity Concept

The basic business unit for which a company keeps separate accounting records and prepares reports is called an ***entity***. An entity may be a person, an organization, a business, or a portion of a business—such as a subsidiary of a corporation. A company can define its own accounting entities. The ***entity concept*** is an accounting principle that states that a company must account separately for the business activities of each business unit. Once the company has identified its accounting entities, only the transactions that concern these entities will typically appear on the company's financial statements.

For example, the Landmark Life Insurance Company is an entity for accounting purposes. Within the entity of Landmark, however, there may be many other entities. If Landmark owns subsidiary companies, and each subsidiary prepares its own financial statements, then each subsidiary is also a separate entity. Further, accounting entities can include Landmark's internal divisions, departments, and lines of business. Typically, a company's divisional or departmental entities maintain detailed records of accounting transactions. These records in turn are summarized and consolidated into the company's financial statements.

To understand and interpret a company's financial statements, you must first be able to identify which entity's accounting information is represented in the financial statements. Usually, the financial statements are labeled with the name of the entity being represented. For example, Landmark's corporate balance sheet would include Landmark Life Insurance Company in the heading. On the other hand, the balance sheet for Landmark's annuity division, which may be a separate entity, would be labeled accordingly.

Going-Concern Concept

The ***going-concern concept*** in accounting requires a company's accounting records to reflect the assumption that the company will continue to operate indefinitely. In other words, the company is not facing liquidation. ***Liquidation*** is the process of selling all company or entity assets, usually to pay off liabilities. The going-concern concept affects a company's financial reporting because this concept

- Allows the company to defer reporting specified costs to a future accounting period if the costs are related to future income
- Assumes that the company will pay off its liabilities over time as scheduled, instead of paying them in full immediately or during the current accounting period

Insurance companies prepare their GAAP-based financial statements according to the going-concern concept or some modification thereof. Figure 3-2 summarizes the entity concept and the going-concern concept.

Accounting Information Qualities

The predictive quality of a company's accounting information can be attributed in part to specified qualities. These qualities include reliability, relevance, consistency, comparability, materiality, and conservatism. These qualities help to ensure that a sophisticated analysis of a company's financial statements will provide an accurate and useful understanding of the company's financial condition. The following sections discuss the impact of these qualities on a company's financial statements.

FIGURE 3-2. Financial Statement Concepts.

Entity concept	Going-concern concept
A company must account separately for the financial transactions of each business unit.	A company maintains its accounting records on the assumption that it will remain in business indefinitely.

Reliability

Accounting information has the quality of ***reliability*** if it is accurate, objective, and free from bias and misrepresentation. Reliable accounting information fairly represents a company's financial strength or profitability. In most situations, objective information is compiled using some standardized measurement method. Further, the company must record and report accounting information in such a manner that outside experts, such as external auditors, can verify that the information is truthful and based on objective measurements. Reliability is perhaps the most important characteristic that accounting information must possess.

Relevance

In accounting terminology, the concept of ***relevance*** requires a company's accounting information to be useful, timely, and likely to affect an interested user's decisions. Relevant accounting information explains how a company has performed during the past accounting period, helps interested users to project how the company is likely to perform in the future, and appears on a timely basis, so that users can act on the information. Only relevant information should be reported in a company's financial statements, because irrelevant information may cloud or distort the picture of the company's financial performance or condition.

Sometimes, however, relevant information is not reliable. For example, information that a company is planning to market a new product is relevant because whether the new product is successful or not could affect an investor's decision to purchase the company's stock. However, information about the financial impact of that new product often reflects management's expectations, not the product's actual performance. Therefore, this information may not be reliable.

Accuracy and independent verification are key components of a company's accounting records and financial statements. For this reason, when relevance and reliability conflict, reliability is typically determined to be more important with respect to reporting financial information. However, the conflict of relevance with reliability does not always lead to a simple choice between these two qualities. Generally, the objective information is reported on an insurer's financial statements, and nonobjective, but relevant, information is reported in an accompanying narrative section of the insurer's financial statements, as shown in Figure 3-3.

Consistency

The principle of ***consistency*** in accounting requires a company to use the same accounting policies and procedures in its financial

FIGURE 3-3. Reliability and Relevance.

The Beacon Life Insurance Company has developed a new annuity product, but has not yet started to sell this product. Information about the new product is relevant. However, Beacon will not include the potential revenues from this product's sales in its financial statements because these revenue amounts are estimates, not actual amounts. Instead, Beacon would include the relevant information on this product's potential revenues in an accompanying note to the financial statements.

On the other hand, Beacon has incurred actual expenses in developing this product. Because the expense amounts are objective, Beacon would include them in its financial statements. In this way, interested users of Beacon's financial information could combine the objective information about new product expenses from Beacon's financial statements with revenue estimates from the accompanying note to forecast the potential impact of the new product on Beacon's future financial statements.

statements from one accounting period to the next, unless there is a sound reason for changing a specified policy or procedure. Consistency has two aspects: a company must (1) record similar transactions the same way from transaction to transaction and (2) report financial information the same way from one accounting period to the next. In some situations, accounting offers more than one acceptable method for assigning a monetary value to an account's balance. An insurer can choose from among several different methods for determining the monetary value of its bond or real estate holdings. The insurer does not have to use the same method for all accounts. For example, the valuation method used for an insurer's bond holdings does not have to be the same valuation method used for an insurer's real estate. However, the method chosen for valuing the insurer's bond holdings or real estate must be applied consistently across accounting periods.

A company can also change the accounting methods it uses from one financial statement to the next, so long as the company describes the financial effects of the change. Why might an insurer decide to change its accounting methods? An insurer typically changes accounting methods as a result of changes in

- Accounting practices or insurance regulations
- The insurer's structure, goals, or procedures
- The insurer's business environment

Comparability

In the context of financial statements, ***comparability*** means that a company's financial statements are presented in such a way that interested users can identify similarities and differences in financial information across accounting periods and among different companies. In other words, a company's financial statements must be comparable both to the company's statements from earlier accounting periods and to the financial statements of other companies for those same accounting periods.

Materiality

The accounting quality of ***materiality*** requires that companies disclose all significant information in their financial statements. Generally, an item of information is material if its disclosure, the lack of its disclosure, or its misrepresentation could lead interested users to change their opinions about the company's financial strength or profitability. Whether information is material or not relies heavily on the judgment of a company's accountants and management. The materiality of information also can vary from company to company. For example, $2,000 of office supplies probably is not a material asset to a $50 billion company, although this same asset probably is material to a one-person company.

Insurers usually consider several factors about a transaction, as well as the types of accounts that the transaction affects, in evaluating the transaction's materiality. Many apparently immaterial items or transactions in isolation may combine to produce a result that is material to—that is, has a profound effect on—a company's financial information. In the United States, the Securities and Exchange Commission has issued a statement that rejects the use of percentage thresholds to determine whether a transaction is material or immaterial, however.

Conservatism

In accounting terminology, ***conservatism*** is a prudent reaction for dealing with uncertainty in accounting records and reports; in practice, the use of conservatism typically understates the values of a company's assets and revenues and overstates the values of the company's liabilities and expenses. By selecting conservative accounting methods, an insurer intends for its policy reserves and surplus to be more than adequate to protect policyowners and beneficiaries from adverse financial conditions. However, insurers apply conservative accounting methods only if such conservatism does not violate more important accounting qualities, such as reliability, consistency, and materiality. Figure 3-4 summarizes the key assumptions that underlie the quality of conservatism.

Figure 3-5 summarizes the important qualities of accounting information.

Accounting Principles

Specific concepts, principles, standards, and guidelines have been developed for all companies to follow in preparing accounting records and financial reports. The following sections discuss these accounting principles and concepts.

Cost Concept

The ***cost concept***, also called the *historical-cost concept*, the *initial-recording concept*, or the *acquisition-cost concept*, is an accounting principle which states that companies should include items on the

FIGURE 3-4. The Quality of Conservatism.

According to conservative accounting practices, a company

- Records revenues only when they are certain
- Records expenses when they are incurred
- Reports losses immediately
- Reports gains only when they actually occur

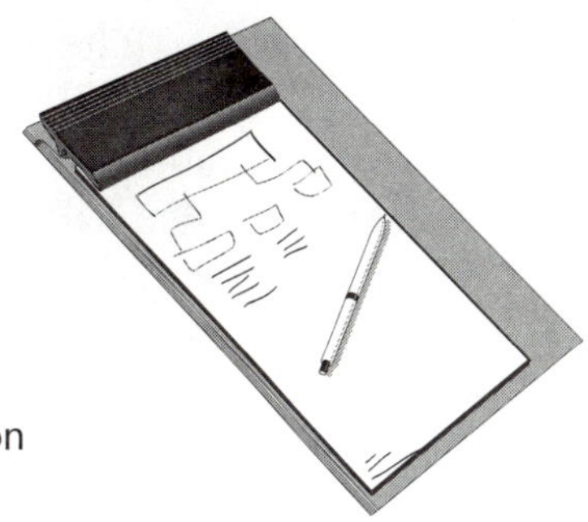

Typically, under conservatism, as compared with other alternative reporting methods, insurers typically use valuations that are based on

- Higher mortality rates for life insurance policies
- Lower mortality rates for annuity contracts
- Higher expense rates for each block of policies
- Lower interest rates for investment earnings on assets that support life insurance policy reserves and annuity reserves

FIGURE 3-5. Qualities of Accounting Information.

Reliability	Accounting records and financial statements present accurate, objective information that is free from bias and misrepresentation
Relevance	Financial statements provide useful and timely information that is likely to affect an interested user's decisions about a company
Consistency	Financial statements apply the same accounting principles and concepts from transaction to transaction over time
Comparability	Financial statements enable analysis within a company and among companies over time
Materiality	Financial statements contain all significant monetary and nonmonetary information
Conservatism	Accounting records and financial statements contain lower monetary values for assets and net income and higher monetary values for expenses and liabilities than would be possible using a less cautious approach to valuation

balance sheet and income statement according to their actual cost at the time of purchase. For example, a company reports the original purchase price, called ***historical cost***, paid for an asset on its balance sheet. On the date of purchase, an asset's historical cost equals its book value. An asset's ***book value*** is the value at which the asset is recorded in a company's accounting records, and this value may change over time.

The reasoning behind the cost concept is that an asset's cost, rather than its current market value, for example, is the most reliable measure of the asset's value. An asset's ***current market value***, also called *fair market value* or simply *market value*, is the price at which the asset can be sold under current economic conditions. Over time, an asset's book value may differ from its historical cost due to a variety of factors, including the asset's current market value. Note that an asset's historical cost may lack relevance because the asset may have significantly increased or decreased in value over time.

Keep in mind, though, that the monetary amount assigned to an asset's current market value may be an estimate. For this reason, current market value would not be a reliable value. However, in other cases, the current market value is known—as in the case of publicly traded common stock—so the asset's value is adjusted to its current market value. Under the cost concept, reliability generally outweighs relevance with respect to the quality of accounting information.

Measuring-Unit Concept

The ***measuring-unit concept*** is an accounting principle which states that a company should record its accounting information in monetary terms, such as U.S. dollars or Canadian dollars. The measuring-unit concept relies upon the assumptions that (1) money is the appropriate unit of measure for business transactions and (2) the measuring unit's value is stable over time.

Full-Disclosure Concept

The ***full-disclosure concept*** is an accounting principle which states that a financial statement must contain all material information about a company and that the company must disclose any additional information or fact that, by its omission, could mislead an interested user of the company's financial information. The full-disclosure concept implies the inclusion of every item that is material, relevant, reliable, and comparable, as well as understandable, to provide a fair representation of a company's financial condition and performance.

The full-disclosure concept points to the critical role of notes and other supplementary materials that accompany an insurer's financial statements. However, the full-disclosure concept does not require the inclusion of excessive details. For example, an independent financial analyst is not better informed about the financial strength of a life insurance company if the company clutters its balance sheet with detailed descriptions of every government security that it owns. In such cases, summary information is more useful.

Time-Period Concept

The ***time-period concept*** is an accounting principle which states that a company's financial statements should report the company's business operations during a specified time period, usually referred to as an accounting period. An accounting period is in itself arbitrary, given the assumed indefinite life associated with the going-concern concept. However, the alternative to artificially imposed accounting periods is to postpone a company's financial statements until the end of the company's life, when all debts are paid and all investor claims are settled. Because a company's financial information is needed during the company's life, the time-period concept has evolved.

The time-period concept assumes that a company can identify an accounting period, reach a suitable cut-off date, and provide summary financial information as of that date or for that period. All companies must file specified financial statements at the end of each one-year period. Most companies also produce financial statements more frequently. Such financial statements are usually referred to as *interim financial statements* to distinguish them from annual financial statements. Typical accounting periods are one month, one quarter, and one year. Most insurance companies use a fiscal year that follows the calendar year—from January through December—as their annual accounting period. A ***fiscal year*** is a 12-month accounting period chosen by a company for financial reporting purposes. The calendar year is the fiscal year for the U.S. Annual Statement and the Canadian Annual Return. Unless specified, a company may select a fiscal year—such as September through August—other than the calendar year for financial reporting purposes.

The drawback to adhering to the time-period concept is that a company does not complete all its transactions within one accounting period. Companies continue to conduct business and make transactions without regard to the artificially imposed accounting period. Because not all transactions are easily identified with a single accounting period, a company's management must ask the question: "When should we record each revenue and each expense?" To help companies answer this question, the accounting profession has developed two principles: (1) the realization principle for revenue recognition and (2) the matching principle for expense recognition.

Revenue Recognition: The Realization Principle

Determining the amount of a company's net income for financial reporting purposes involves both revenue recognition and expense recognition. In accounting terminology, ***recognition*** refers to the process of classifying an item in a financial statement as an asset, liability, owners' equity, revenue, or expense. Generally, a company recognizes revenue when a product is sold, when a service is completed, when cash changes hands, or when the legal ownership of a product passes from the company to a customer as part of a business transaction.

An insurer does not necessarily receive all its revenues in the same accounting period in which it earns them. For this reason, the insurer follows certain guidelines to match the revenue with its correct accounting period, which is the period during which the insurer has earned the revenue. Under GAAP, the ***realization principle*** states that a company should recognize revenue when it is earned, regardless of when the company receives the actual payment, so long as a legal and reasonable expectation exists that the customer will remit payment in full. For life insurance companies, revenue recognition applies primarily to the receipt of life insurance premiums or annuity considerations. Insurers recognize insurance premiums as they are earned over the lifetime of the insurance policy or annuity contract. Figure 3-6 presents an example of how a life insurer would recognize premium income under the realization principle.

Expense Recognition: The Matching Principle

The matching principle governs the recognition of expenses. The ***matching principle*** is a GAAP expense recognition concept which states that a company should recognize expenses as the company

FIGURE 3-6. The Realization Principle.

The Big Corporation signs a contract with the Friendly Life Insurance Company for a group life insurance policy that will provide coverage to Big's employees from January 1, 2001, through December 31, 2001. The annual premiums for this policy are $36,000, payable by Big in quarterly installments of $9,000.

Big decides to prepay the entire $36,000 annual premium on January 1, 2001. On March 31, 2001, Friendly will have earned premium income for only the first quarter—January through March—of the year, even though Friendly has received payment for the entire year.

Although Friendly expects that it will eventually earn the entire annual premium, it has not yet provided the necessary coverage. Therefore, on its March 31, 2001, income statement, Friendly recognizes only $9,000, the first quarter's premium income on this policy. Below is a table that shows when Friendly will recognize the premium income it received from Big.

Income Statement for the Quarter Ended:	Revenue Recognition	Amount
March 31, 2001	January 1—March 31, 2001	$9,000
June 30, 2001	April 1—June 30, 2001	$9,000
September 30, 2001	July 1—September 30, 2001	$9,000
December 31, 2001	October 1—December 31, 2001	$9,000
	Total	$36,000

Suppose Friendly incurred $6,500 of expenses for Big's insurance coverage during the January 1—March 31, 2001 quarter. In this case, Friendly would recognize the $6,500 of incurred expenses with the $9,000 of earned revenue during this accounting period.

earns the revenues related to those expenses, regardless of when the company receives payment for the revenues earned. The realization principle and the matching principle work in tandem. A company reports earned revenue under the realization principle. The company also identifies the expenses it incurred to earn that specified revenue and records these expenses under the matching principle. GAAP generally permits three approaches to expense recognition: (1) associating cause and effect, (2) systematic and rational allocation, and (3) immediate recognition. Figure 3-7 defines and provides examples of these three approaches.

Figure 3-8 summarizes the principles, concepts, and guidelines that all companies comply with for financial accounting purposes.

Accounting Bases

The application of both the realization principle and the matching principle depend in part on the accounting basis used by a company in maintaining accounting records and preparing financial statements. The following sections discuss two accounting bases: (1) accrual-basis accounting and (2) cash-basis accounting.

Accrual-Basis Accounting

Under ***accrual-basis accounting***, a company records revenues when they are earned and expenses when they are incurred, even if the company has not yet received the revenues or paid the expenses. Accrual-basis accounting records revenues according to the realization principle and expenses according to the matching principle. Accrual-basis accounting helps to match expenses with revenues, a process that typically enables companies to develop more relevant, reliable, and comparable financial statements. The purpose of accrual-basis accounting is to record a business transaction when a company incurs a financial obligation either as the payer or the payee. Thus, accrual-basis accounting enables interested users of a company's financial information to view the consequences of a company's actions or activities. For this reason, accrual-basis accounting is generally regarded as more relevant than cash-basis accounting. FASB (U.S.) and the CICA (Canada) mandate the use of accrual-basis accounting for financial reporting purposes.

Two separate accounting records of a business transaction often result from the use of accrual-basis accounting: (1) the first accounting entry recognizes the revenue earned or the expenses incurred, and (2) the second accounting entry recognizes the revenue received or the expenses disbursed. Accrual-basis accounting provides information on the consequences of a company's business transactions,

FIGURE 3-7. Three Approaches to Expense Recognition.

Associating Cause and Effect

Under statutory accounting, life insurers generally recognize all incurred expenses in the current accounting period, rather than spread these expenses over the accounting periods in which premium income is earned. However, under GAAP, some expenses may be deferred and recognized over time. According to ***associating cause and effect***, expenses that have a direct relationship to specified future revenues are charged to future accounting periods instead of being charged to the current accounting period. Agent commissions is an example of an expense that has a direct relationship to premium income. Under GAAP, for specified types of insurance products, a life insurance company recognizes agent commissions in the same accounting period in which it receives the premium income generated by this expense. However, the expenses associated with products such as investment contracts and participating policies are usually spread across accounting periods as profits emerge from these products.

For example, the Heraldic Life Insurance Company incurred agent commissions of $500,000 this year for its participating products. Under statutory accounting practices, Heraldic would report the entire $500,000 expense for agent commissions this year. Under GAAP, however, Heraldic would have to report only that portion of the $500,000 expense that applied directly to premium income earned this year. Heraldic calculates the amount to recognize as an expense each year according to the relationship of the current year's earned premium income to its estimated future years' premium income for its participating products.

Systematic and Rational Allocation

Sometimes a direct association of cause and effect between revenues and expenses is not clearly recognizable. In such cases, a company uses another approach to expense recognition. Under ***systematic and rational allocation***, a company expenses an asset's cost over its estimated useful life, regardless of when the company receives revenues from the asset. A common example of systematic and rational allocation is depreciation. ***Depreciation*** is the process of spreading (allocating) the cost of an asset over the asset's estimated useful life.

For example, suppose Heraldic purchases a new computer system for $1,000,000. Heraldic's management does not know for certain how long it will own the system. Futhermore, expenses that Heraldic incurred for the system and the revenues Heraldic hopes to generate from selling life insurance policies are not directly related. Heraldic estimates that the useful life of the new computer system is eight years and that the systems salvage value is $200,000. An asset's ***salvage value*** is the residual value or selling price of the asset at the end of its useful life. To calculate the depreciation on the system, Heraldic will report $100,000 in depreciation [($1,000,000 cost – $200,000 salvage value) ÷ 8 years] during each year of the system's estimated life.

Immediate Recognition

Sometimes a company cannot match expenses during an accounting period with revenues earned for that period, nor can it match the expenses with revenues it expects to generate in the future. Some expenses that a company incurs cannot be directly matched with revenues. Other incurred expenses may provide no objectively recognizable future benefits to the company. In such cases, the company uses the immediate recognition approach to reporting expenses. Under ***immediate recognition***, a company recognizes all costs as expenses during the current accounting period. Immediate expense recognition is common under statutory reporting requirements.

For example, suppose Heraldic incurs $35,000 in expenses for general legal services that cannot be attributed to revenues earned. Under both GAAP and statutory accounting, Heraldic reports the entire $35,000 expense during the current accounting period. Heraldic incurs $12,000 in employee training costs, which it also treats as a current expense because Heraldic cannot attribute this expense to a specific amount of earned revenue.

FIGURE 3-8. Principles for Maintaining Accounts.

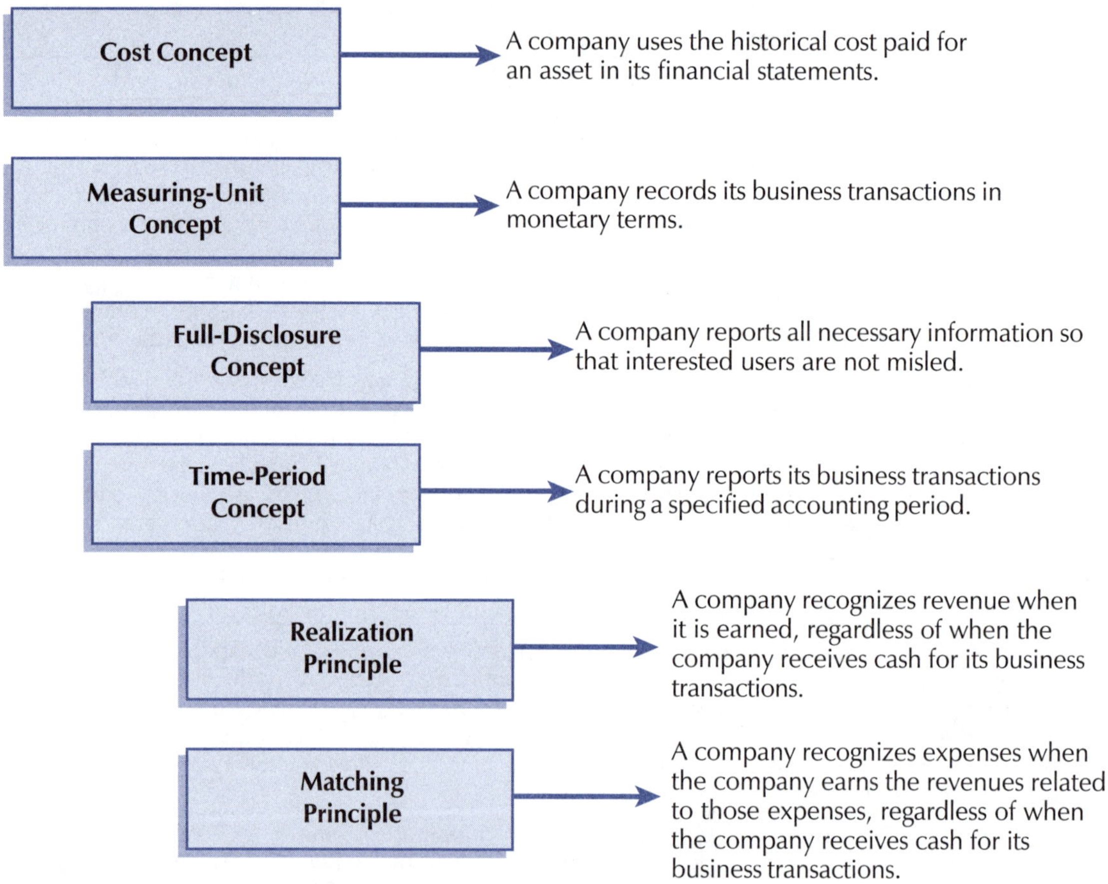

including the company's earning potential and financial performance. Companies that use accrual-basis accounting must also make adjusting entries to their accounting records at the end of each accounting period to match revenues and expenses in their financial statements for that accounting period.

Cash-Basis Accounting

Cash-basis accounting is a system in which a company recognizes revenues or expenses only when it receives or disburses cash. Neither the realization principle nor the matching principle applies under cash-basis accounting. Instead, cash receipts and cash disbursements are the most important components of cash-basis accounting. In contrast, under accrual-basis accounting, a company's financial statements must report the results of both cash and non-cash transactions, such as purchases on account, that occur during the accounting period.

A ***cash receipt*** is a check, money order, electronic funds transfer (EFT), or other cash transaction that is remitted to a company as a form of payment for goods or services rendered. A company records a cash receipt in the same accounting period in which it receives the cash. A ***cash disbursement*** is the payment of cash by a company to a beneficiary or other payee. Under cash-basis accounting, a company records a cash disbursement in the same accounting period in which it remits payment. In a pure cash-basis system, a company makes no accounting entries to record pending revenues or expenses. Instead, the company calculates its net income by subtracting paid expenses from received revenues.

Figure 3-9 compares, for a specified business transaction, the accounting entries that a company would make under accrual-basis accounting and cash-basis accounting.

Because cash-basis accounting does not apply the realization principle or the matching principle, misleading financial statements can result. For example, under cash-basis accounting, Principium's balance sheet of December 31, 2001, would not show that the balance in Principium's Office Equipment account has increased by $50,000, nor would it show that Principium owes Functional $50,000

FIGURE 3-9. Accounting Entries: Accrual-Basis and Cash-Basis.

On December, 31, 2001, the last day of its annual accounting period, the Principium Life Insurance Company purchased $50,000 of office equipment on account from the Functional Office Equipment Company. That same day, Functional delivers the equipment to Principium. Principium remits payment in full on January 10, 2002. Below are the accounting entries for this transaction, under accrual-basis accounting and cash-basis accounting.

	Cash-Basis	Accrual-Basis
December 31, 2001		*Debit* Office Equipment $50,000 *Credit* Accounts Payable $50,000
January 10, 2002	*Debit* Office Equipment $50,000 *Credit* Cash $50,000	*Debit* Accounts Payable $50,000 *Credit* Cash $50,000

for the new office equipment. However, this transaction may be material to Principium's potential policyowners or investors. In contrast, under accrual-basis accounting, Principium's balance sheet would show the financial effect of this transaction.

Traditionally, life insurance companies in the United States accounted for their financial transactions under both statutory accounting and GAAP, by using cash-basis accounting for the initial premium, for example. Then, to prepare financial statements, insurers in the United States made adjusting entries from the cash basis to the accrual basis for some items. Today, accounting software enables insurers to maintain their accounting records simultaneously on both a cash basis and an accrual basis.

Key Terms and Concepts

predictive quality
entity
entity concept
going-concern concept
liquidation
reliability
relevance
consistency
comparability
materiality
conservatism
cost concept
historical cost
book value
current market value
measuring-unit concept
full-disclosure concept
time-period concept
fiscal year
recognition
realization principle
matching principle
associating cause and effect
systematic and rational allocation
depreciation
salvage value
immediate recognition
accrual-basis accounting
cash-basis accounting
cash receipt
cash disbursement

Chapter 4

Internal Control and Auditing

Chapter Outline

Internal Control

- Detective Controls and Preventive Controls
- Limitations of Internal Controls
- Compliance and Monitoring
- Principles of Effective Internal Control

Auditing

- Internal Auditing
- External Auditing
- Auditor Opinions

OBJECTIVES

After reading this chapter, you should be able to

- List the primary goals of internal control
- Recognize the key principles of an effective system of internal controls
- Differentiate between internal auditing and external auditing
- Identify the primary types of internal auditing and external auditing

The activities associated with accounting and financial reporting are an integral part of an insurer's control function, which serves to measure and to monitor an insurer's transactions as it pursues its corporate objectives, such as solvency, profitability, and quality service to policyowners. Two key aspects of an insurer's control function that directly affect all insurance operations are internal control and financial auditing.

Internal control consists of the steps a company takes to (1) protect its assets, (2) monitor the accuracy of its accounting records, and (3) encourage both operational efficiency and adherence to the company's management policies. ***Financial auditing*** (auditing) is the process of examining and evaluating company records and procedures to ensure that (1) the company's accounting records and financial statements are presented fairly and reasonably, (2) quality assurance is maintained, and (3) operational procedures and policies are effective.

Financial auditing may be conducted on an internal or external basis. Although not all audits are financial audits, in this chapter we are primarily interested in financial audits. Therefore, in this text, when we use the terms *auditing* and *audit*, we mean *financial auditing* and *financial audit*. An ***audit*** (financial audit) is an evaluation of whether a company's financial information, financial statements, and source documents comply with accounting standards and are a fair and consistent depiction of the company's financial condition and performance.

Typically, the internal control and auditing functions are separate from the duties of the accounting department. To perform their analysis effectively and without bias, audit and control personnel must maintain a high degree of independence and objectivity regarding other departments. Figure 4-1 shows examples of specific activities for which insurers establish internal controls and which internal and external auditors review.

Chapter 4 discusses internal controls, including specific types of accounting controls, the advantages and limitations of internal controls, the elements of effective control, and examples of internal controls. We also discuss internal and external auditing, including financial auditing, compliance auditing, and performance auditing.

Internal Control

Internal controls are divided into two general types: administrative controls and accounting controls. ***Administrative controls*** are the policies and procedures that guide employees in conducting their normal

FIGURE 4-1. Insurance Activities and the Control Function.

Functional Area	Internal Controls and Auditing ensure that . . .
Premium Income	• Duties for premium collection and premium accounting are segregated. • Premium notices have correct premium amounts. • Preauthorized checks (PACs) and electronic funds transfers (EFTs) have proper authorization and correct amounts. • The policyowner master file has current and correct policy paid-to dates. • Procedures are established for advance premiums, automatic premium loans (APLs), policy lapses, and policy surrenders.
Reinsurance	• Reinsurance is obtained in accordance with the insurer's retention limits. • Reinsurers are billed promptly for recoverable benefits. • Ceding company records are routinely compared with reinsurer records.
Agent Commissions	• Procedures for determining agent balances due are established. • Procedures for proper authorization and accurate payment of agent commissions on individual and group insurance products are followed. • Commission payments are routinely compared with premium income and insurance company products. • Chargeback procedures for agent commissions upon policy lapse or policy surrender are established.
Policy Reserves	• Adequate policy reserves are maintained. • Reserve valuation procedures comply with regulatory requirements and applicable accounting principles and practices. • Routine comparisons of in-force policies and the reserves for each policy type are conducted.
Benefit Payments	• Duties for claim processing and claim disbursement are segregated. • Proper authorization and approval of benefit payments are documented. • Disbursement records are compared routinely with prenumbered checks. • Approved claims and claim disbursements are reconciled routinely.
Treasury Operations (cash management)	• Duties for cash receipts, cash disbursements, and bank reconciliation are segregated. • Collections procedures are efficient. • Management of cash flows is effective and efficient. • Appropriate and consistent controls for authorization, check security, and accounting records for cash disbursements are maintained.

Source: *LOMA Internal Audit Manual*, 7th ed. (Atlanta: LOMA, 1995), various pages.

day-to-day tasks. An example of an administrative control is a policy that requires a manager to check business references before hiring a new employee.

Accounting controls are the policies and procedures used to authorize financial transactions, safeguard assets, and provide reliable, timely, and fairly presented financial information about a company. Accounting controls in insurance companies generally include the preparation and analysis of financial statements, internal auditing, and other measures of financial performance. By adhering to accounting controls, an insurer can be reasonably certain that only authorized employees

- Record accounting entries for the insurer's financial transactions
- Prepare financial statements that comply with applicable accounting principles and regulatory requirements
- Access the insurer's assets
- Compare the insurer's assets with its accounting records for those assets

Although administrative controls and accounting controls have unique qualities, they are sometimes difficult to distinguish in practice. The American Institute of Certified Public Accountants (AICPA) has stated that the two types of internal control are not necessarily mutually exclusive. This chapter focuses on accounting controls that are associated with financial reporting.

Generally, internal controls are designed to prevent or reduce losses arising from (1) mistakes or irregularities in transaction processing and asset handling and (2) unexpected losses or contingencies. Determining the risk level associated with various types of losses and developing safeguards to manage the risk of loss are key responsibilities of an insurance company's management team.

Detective Controls and Preventive Controls

An insurer's internal controls should include both detective and preventive controls. A ***detective control*** is an internal control that identifies an error or problem after it has occurred. Most detective controls are undertaken after a series of business transactions. A ***preventive control*** is an internal control that is designed to keep an error or a problem from occurring. Normally, preventive controls involve steps that must be taken before a business transaction occurs. Figure 4-2 lists examples of detective controls and preventive controls in insurance companies.

Preventive controls are usually more effective at reducing errors or problems than are detective controls, but preventive controls are

FIGURE 4-2. Detective Controls and Preventive Controls.

Detective Controls

- Claims disbursements are reviewed monthly
- Department accounts are balanced daily
- Reports of questionable data are reviewed daily

Preventive Controls

- Proper authorization is required before claims processors disburse benefit payments
- Two signatures are required on checks written over a specified dollar amount
- Only valid codes are allowed to be entered for each transaction

also typically more expensive. As with any other expense, insurers analyze both preventive and detective controls to ensure that they provide benefits that are worth their costs. Detective controls and preventive controls can be applied as administrative controls or accounting controls.

Limitations of Internal Controls

Internal controls are a necessary part of a life insurance company's operations. However, no system of internal controls is infallible. Internal controls are designed for specified conditions. As these conditions change, the internal controls must also be changed. External changes such as amendments to the federal income tax code and accounting practices or internal changes such as the introduction of a new product and the modification of an existing product may mandate the need for a review of the company's internal controls. The following sections discuss two common limitations of internal controls.

Employee Errors

An insurance company's internal controls are designed in part to reduce or avoid employee errors. However, employees can make mistakes in implementing the internal controls. Improperly implemented controls are unlikely to detect the problems they were designed to detect. Common approaches to managing the problem of employee errors are for a company to (1) hire the best qualified people available, (2) train new employees thoroughly in the proper use of established internal controls, and (3) involve experienced employees in the development of new internal controls.

Criminal Acts

Internal controls are also designed to reduce the incidence of criminal acts such as theft against a company by employees. Because no system is perfect, however, a determined employee can occasionally circumvent a company's internal controls, at least temporarily. A company must examine and evaluate its policies and procedures, then develop controls that fit the company's operations. Internal controls must be workable from an operational point of view as well as provide greater benefits than they cost.

Compliance and Monitoring

A company's internal control system must facilitate employee training, facilitate communication of policies and procedures, serve as warning signals for prompt error detection, and indicate whether the company is complying with regulatory requirements. An insurer could be subject to fines and other penalties for noncompliance with regulatory requirements.

For example, regulators can impose a fine on a life insurance company that continues to file late quarterly financial statements. The payment of fines and penalties decreases an insurer's net income and ultimately its surplus. To minimize the risk of noncompliance, insurers implement a strong system of internal controls. Some insurers have a compliance officer or a cross-divisional team of employees to monitor compliance issues.

Principles of Effective Internal Control

The following sections summarize some critical principles that are common to an effective internal control system.

Segregation of Duties

The principle of ***segregation of duties***, also known as the principle of *dual control*, requires an employer to design jobs so that incompatible functions are assigned to different individuals. In this context, ***incompatible functions*** are job duties that, when combined, place an employee in a position to commit an illegal act or to conceal errors or irregularities in the normal course of his or her employment. Segregating duties among employees provides an environment in which an insurer can safeguard its assets and detect and correct errors and irregularities quickly.

Generally, an effective internal control system separates the (1) custodial tasks, (2) authorization tasks, and (3) accounting tasks associated with an insurer's assets. In this context, *custody* is defined as the physical or electronic handling of assets. Therefore, an investment department employee who assumes custody—whether physical or electronic—of securities should not be the same employee who maintains the accounting records associated with these securities, nor should either of those employees be authorized to sell or otherwise dispose of these securities.

Complicating an insurer's adherence to the segregation of duties is the trend toward employee empowerment, especially start-to-finish processing by one employee. Under employee empowerment programs, many insurers delegate authority to employees at the lowest possible level in specified functions. Sometimes this delegation results in a blurring of incompatible functions. The existence of employee empowerment programs therefore requires insurers to conduct random internal audits of an insurer's business transactions more frequently than in a more hierarchical organization.

Insurers often purchase a fidelity bond on each employee who oversees particularly sensitive areas such as investment management or cash management (treasury operations). A ***fidelity bond*** is an indemnity insurance agreement guaranteeing to the purchaser the coverage of a financial loss caused by (1) the act or default of a third party, such as an employee, or (2) some contingency, such as fire, over which the third party may have no control. Fidelity bonds help to protect the insurer from the risks associated with employee violation of internal controls. Some insurance companies purchase fidelity bonds on all employees.

Execution of Transactions as Authorized

The ***execution of transactions as authorized*** is the element of the internal control system that concerns the delegation of authority to perform specified tasks and the communication of that authority. In an insurance company, many different types of monetary transactions—such as purchasing and selling securities, issuing policies, paying benefits, and paying operating expenses—require employee authorization. No financial transaction should occur without some form of official authorization.

Authorization levels should be realistic and a company should communicate them clearly. An ***authorization level*** is the maximum monetary amount that a company employee has been granted official power to approve for disbursement. Whatever the type of transaction, a specified employee authorizes each transaction at the appropriate level. Each authorization level should reflect the transaction and the experience and responsibility of the employee concerned. For example, a claims processor with only two months' work experience may have to obtain authorization for all claim payments over $2,500, although an experienced claims processor may be authorized to approve claim payments up to $50,000, within specified guidelines.

Recording of Transactions as Executed

The ***recording of transactions as executed*** means that a company records all authorized and executed transactions in the correct accounting period, in the correct accounts, and in the correct monetary amounts. In this way, the company can summarize all transactions for that accounting period in its financial statements. Suppose an insurer records premium income when it is received. The accounting entry includes the proper amount of the cash receipt as posted to the correct record in the policyowner master file and the correct bank account. Communicating the policies and procedures necessary to document a financial transaction is an essential part of recording transactions as executed. Employee training sessions, prenumbered checks and purchase orders, and written procedures manuals help to support the documentation of an insurer's financial transactions.

Safeguarding of Assets

The ***safeguarding of assets*** is the process of (1) limiting access to offices, documents, and records; (2) storing negotiable documents in vaults to which no person has sole access; (3) maintaining written business disaster recovery plans and off-premises storage of back-up files for all critical records; (4) investigating the integrity of employees hired to fill sensitive positions; (5) taking a physical inventory of all assets and comparing this count to a written record; and (6) reviewing the adequacy of insurance coverage, given a company's risk exposure.

Safeguarding assets requires sensitive handling. Specified assets need to be sufficiently accessible so that a company can easily conduct its normal business operations. The company should restrict access to these assets to authorized persons. Threats to an insurer's assets include theft, destruction, waste, and deterioration. An insurer's computer system may be safeguarded, for example, by

- Requiring the use of passwords before users are allowed access to software applications
- Restricting access to the system's physical location

- Maintaining adequate property and liability insurance and service contracts on the system
- Requiring employees to follow appropriate virus protection procedures
- Providing back-up copies of critical records and housing them in an off-site facility
- Separating the incompatible functions between those who program the database software and those who enter records into the database

Physical Comparison of Recorded Amounts

The ***physical comparison of recorded amounts*** means that a company counts its assets, revenues, and expenses on a periodic basis and compares this count to the amounts in its accounting records. This physical comparison is typically accomplished by means of an inventory. An ***inventory*** is an itemized count and listing of a company's assets, such as property, products, materials, or securities.

Figure 4-3 lists several common examples of different types of internal controls that you may find in an insurance company.

Auditing

All insurance companies undergo periodic internal and external accounting audits or examinations. Internal auditors are company employees and the audits they perform are known as internal audits. An ***internal audit*** is a type of internal control that is performed by company employees who assess and evaluate the company's internal controls. An ***external audit*** is performed by external auditors, who are employed by public accounting firms or insurance regulators.

The overall purpose of an audit is to gather information that either supports or refutes an assertion. Both internal and external auditors typically have the following responsibilities:

- Verifying that a company's assets are accounted for and that they are safeguarded from loss
- Assessing the soundness and the application of the company's administrative and accounting controls
- Ensuring that employees follow specified policies and procedures
- Verifying the reliability of the company's accounting records and financial reports
- Evaluating the effectiveness and efficiency of specified operating procedures

FIGURE 4-3. Examples of Internal Controls.

Approval, review, checking, or recalculation

- Senior management approves all claims payments over a specified dollar amount
- Actuarial staff recalculates premiums charged on a block of policies
- Claims processors complete a checklist that indicates the insurer has received all required documents before the insurer pays a claim or approves a policy loan

Comparing information on independently generated documents

- Underwriting staff compares information from a policy application with the policyowner master file
- Customer service staff compares the monetary amount of a policy loan requested by a policyowner with the amount on the loan check before mailing the check

Prenumbering

- Checks and purchase orders are printed with sequential numbers
- Policy applications and claims are numbered as they are received
- Internal auditors check the numbering sequence and reconcile any number that is missing or out of sequence

Maintenance of control totals

- All policy loans are listed and subtotaled separately, then the subtotals are reconciled to the insurer's total policy loans
- Premium checks are grouped and totaled to obtain a batch total, which is entered into the insurer's automated system

Comparison with third-party information

- The insurer's cash receipts and disbursements are reconciled with the insurer's bank statement
- Investment staff reconcile internally generated lists of securities held in safekeeping with lists provided by the insurer's depository or custodian
- Information in the insurer's accounting records concerning its notes payable is reconciled with statements provided by the notes' owners
- Requests for notification of errors in payments or policy records or confirmation of amounts receivable from persons or companies that owe the insurer money are routinely compared

Cancellation of documentation

- Cancelled or voided documents are defaced or shredded in some way so they cannot be sent through normal channels of processing

Timeliness of operation

- All transactions are processed promptly, including daily deposits of cash receipts and periodic reviews of new business to resolve insurance policies that have neither been issued nor denied after a specified time

Specifically, an insurer undertakes an audit to determine the degree of correlation between specific standards and the insurer's financial and operational actions and to communicate the results of the audit to interested users of the insurer's financial information. Figure 4-4 lists potential areas of an insurance company that are subject to audits.

Auditors review an insurer's records in part to uncover unintentional errors or false information in the insurer's accounting records and financial statements. Auditors also examine evidence of ***fraud***, which is the intentional use of false information to mislead another party. Although an insurer's internal controls may be effective against fraud committed by one person, they may be less effective at detecting fraud that arises from collusion. ***Collusion*** is a secret agreement entered into by two or more persons to perpetrate an illegal act. Collusion is used to circumvent controls such as segregation of duties or authorization levels.

One audit device is an ***audit trail***, which is a chronological, sequential set of accounting records and reports from the beginning to the end of a business transaction. Auditing provides the opportunity for an auditor to isolate any breach of control and bring it to the attention of the insurer and/or regulators. By examining an insurer's audit trails for a variety of financial transactions, an auditor can also identify the overall strengths and weaknesses of the insurer's system of internal controls.

Examining every accounting entry to verify each financial transaction would be impractical and costly. Instead, auditors rely on a system of statistical sampling in which they examine a portion of the company's accounts, transactions, and operations. Samples are chosen according to sound statistical methods, which provide auditors with a reasonable level of confidence that all the company's accounts, transactions, and operations are as valid as those in the sample. In many cases, an auditor reviews transactions at only two or three key points in the process. Such a review indicates whether related transactions have been processed similarly.

Next, we discuss the contrasting purposes of internal auditing and external auditing.

Internal Auditing

Typically, internal audits focus on an insurer's (1) accounting records and financial statements, (2) regulatory compliance, (3) external auditor findings, (4) tax reporting, and (5) operating efficiency with respect to company policies and procedures. An insurer's internal auditing function may be organized by regional office, distribution system, or by line of business. To conduct a thorough internal audit,

FIGURE 4-4. Potential Areas for Insurance Company Audits.

Note: The following list is not intended to be a complete listing of areas in a life insurance company that are subject to audits. The list is shown, however, as a representative example.

Financial Division

Bank Reconciliation
Bonds and Stocks
Dividends Received on Stocks
Home Office Building and Real Estate
Interest Received on Bonds
Mortgage Loans
Petty Cash
Real Estate Purchased for Income
Security Vault Control
Separate Accounts

Ordinary Division

Accident and Health Reserves
Agency Expense Allowance
Agents' Benefit Plans
Agents' Financing
Commissions Due and Unpaid
Commissions Paid
Contractual Reserves
Death Claims Paid
Death Claims Due and Unpaid
Disability Claims
Dividend Accumulations
Dividends Paid to Policyowners
Inspection Report Fees
Medical Examination Fees
Periodic Annuity Payments
Policyowner Master File
Policy Loans
Premiums
Surrender Benefits

Other

Agency Offices
Equity Investments
Mortgage Loan Correspondents
Subsidiaries

Group Division

Accident and Health Benefits
Accident and Health Claims
Agency Expense Allowance
Agents Benefit Plans
Agents' Financing
Claim Drafts Payable
Commissions Due and Unpaid
Commissions Paid
Contingency Reserve
Contractual Reserves
Death Claims
Death Claims Due and Unpaid
Commissions Paid
Contingency Reserve
Death Claims
Death Claims Due and Unpaid
Dividends to Policyowners
Inspection Report Fees
Medical Examination Fees
Periodic Annuity Payments
Premiums
Service Fees
Unearned Premium Reserves—Accident and Health

Corporate

Advertising
Employee Benefit Plans
Furniture and Equipment
Home Office Budgets
Information Systems
Loans
Operating Expenses
Payroll
Postage and Expenses
Rent Paid
Rental of Equipment
Stock
Taxes
Telephone
Travel

Source: *Establishing an Internal Audit Function in a Life Insurance Company*, Financial Planning and Control Report No. 24 (New York: LOMA, 1972), 32.

internal auditors may need to consult with a specialist in specified technical areas.

Figure 4-5 is a flowchart of general activities typically involved in an internal audit.

Although internal audits are not required by law or by regulations in the United States and Canada, most companies conduct them as a preventive measure, to uncover potential problems, or to discover ideas for improving a particular process. To remain objective, a company's internal auditors should have unrestricted access to all records, procedures, files, and reports that concern the scope of the audit, and they should not directly supervise nor report to the areas they audit. Further, internal auditors usually report to a senior-level executive or to the audit committee of the insurer's board of directors.

FIGURE 4-5. Internal Audit Activities.

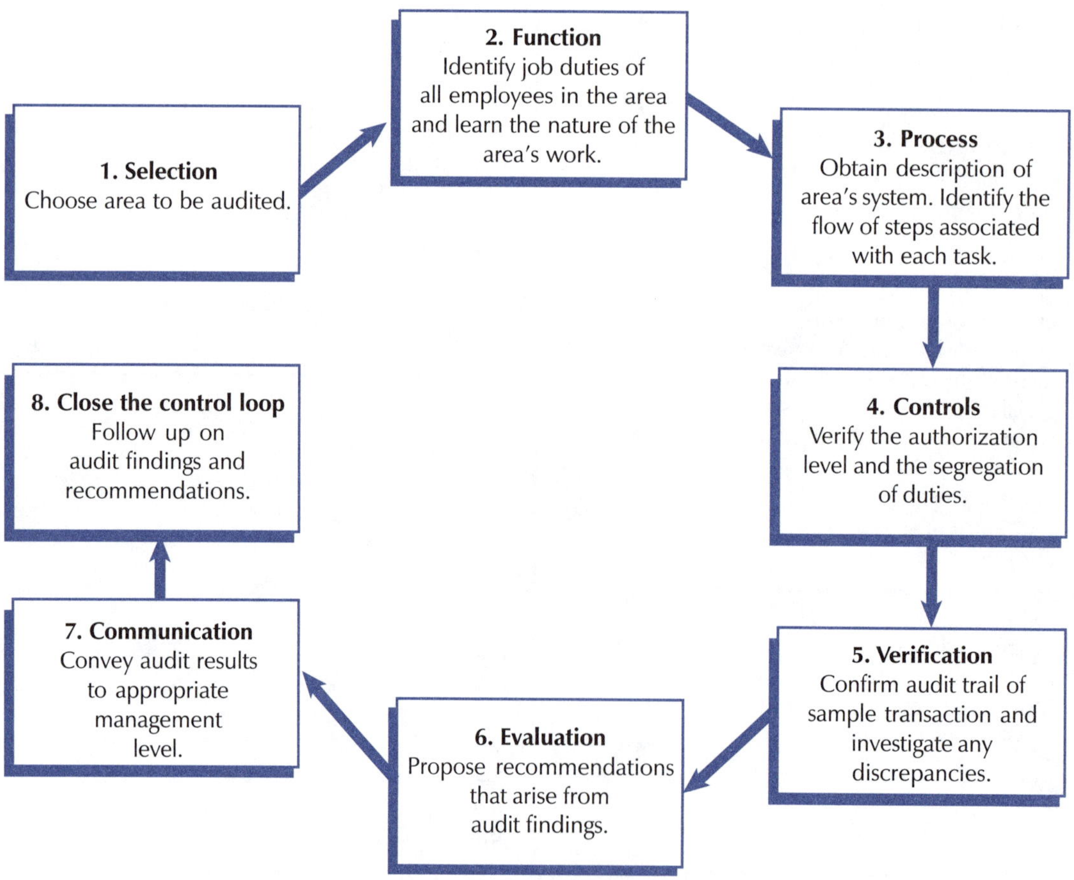

Source: *Establishing an Internal Audit Function in a Life Insurance Company*, Financial Planning and Control Report No. 24 (New York: LOMA, 1972), 13–14.

In the United States, a company's internal auditors must comply with generally accepted auditing standards (GAAS) established by the American Institute of Certified Public Accountants (AICPA). Canadian auditors typically comply with generally accepted auditing standards developed by the Canadian Institute of Chartered Accountants (CICA).

External Auditing

The purposes of an external audit or examination are to (1) issue an opinion as to whether a company's financial statements present fairly, in all material respects, the company's operations through adherence to a given set of accounting standards, (2) review and recommend changes to the company's system of internal control, and (3) prepare reports of audit findings. An external audit is conducted primarily for the benefit of interested third parties, including an insurer's board of directors, shareholders, policyowners, creditors, and regulators. Figure 4-6 presents a flowchart of the typical external audit process.

All publicly traded companies in the United States and all federally licensed companies in Canada are required to contract with independent external auditors—typically a public accounting firm—to perform annual audits of financial information that is included in the annual report. The use of independent auditors helps to ensure that a company's financial performance is evaluated objectively. Typically, an insurer's external audit focuses on accounting and financial reporting functions, including the insurer's solvency, regulatory compliance, and tax reporting.

All insurance companies also undergo periodic regulatory examinations, which are a specific type of external audit. For example, the National Association of Insurance Commissioners (NAIC) conducts an on-site examination every three to five years—depending on the state and the insurer's financial condition—of each insurance company in the United States. This type of external audit typically includes the examination of a company's (1) financial statements, (2) individual accounts and accounting records, and (3) source documents for the accounting records. If an insurer is having financial difficulties, an annual examination may be conducted. In Canada, the Office of the Superintendent of Financial Institutions (OSFI) conducts such examinations.

Auditor Opinions

External auditors also prepare and sign the auditor's opinion or report that is found at the end of a company's annual report. An ***auditor's opinion*** is a statement, prepared by an independent public accounting

FIGURE 4-6. Flowchart of an External Audit.

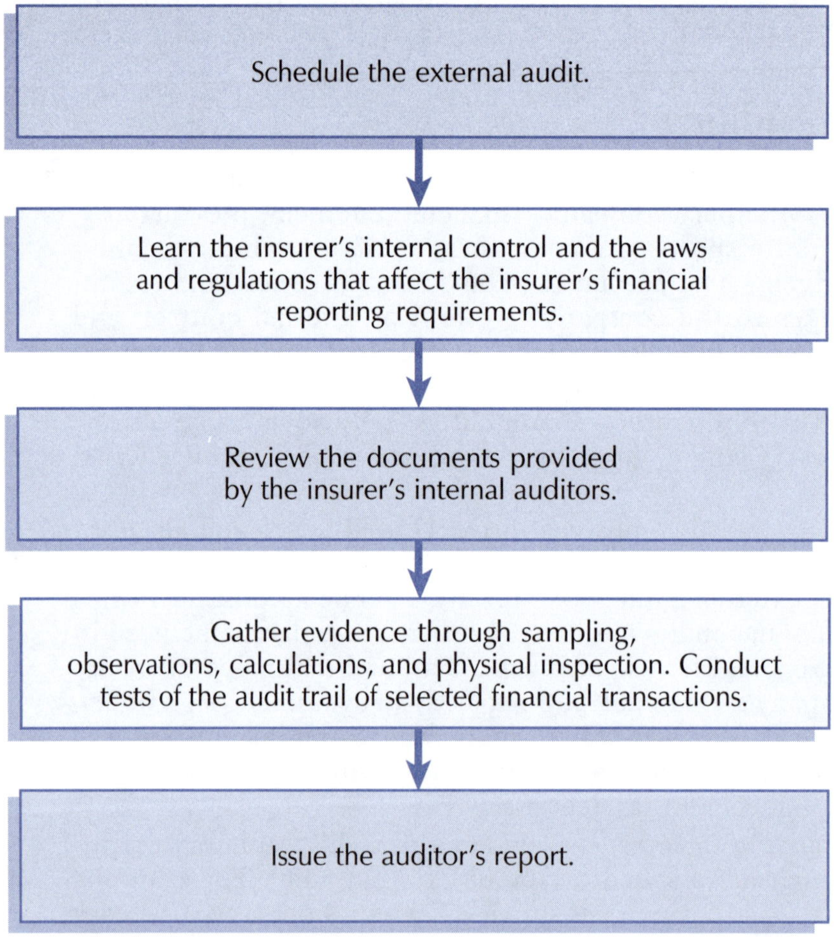

Source: Adapted from *Reports Prepared by Chartered Accountants—What Do They Mean?* (Toronto: Chartered Accountants of Canada), p. 4.

company, that attests that the information contained in the company's annual report fairly represents the operations of the company and that the audit was conducted in accordance with generally accepted auditing standards (GAAS). An auditor's opinion does not, however, guarantee the accuracy of the financial statements. It simply indicates whether the annual report appears to offer a fair representation of the company's financial position and operations in accordance with accounting standards, such as GAAP.

Auditors conclude a company's annual report with one of several different types of auditor's opinions. The type of auditor's opinion that companies prefer is an unqualified opinion. However, because of numerous regulatory and industry changes in accounting principles and practices, the incidence of modified opinions has increased. Under certain circumstances, neither an unqualified opinion nor a modified opinion is possible. Instead, a non-standard auditor's opinion is required. Figure 4-7 summarizes the different types of auditor's opinions for companies in the United States and Canada.

FIGURE 4-7. Types of Auditor's Opinions.

United States

- **Unqualified opinion** (standard report or clean opinion): Indicates that the financial statements present fairly, in all material respects, the financial position, results of operations, and cash flows of the entity in conformity with GAAP or, for "special purpose" financial statements, in accordance with statutory accounting practices
- **Modified opinion** (modified unqualified consistency report): Contains explanatory language concerning specific circumstances, such as material inconsistencies resulting from a change in accounting principles or practices

Non-standard auditor's reports:

- **Qualified opinion:** States the area of exception to an otherwise unqualified opinion (for example, the insurer has a large pending lawsuit for a disputed claim for which the amount of the claim liability is material and under contention)
- **Adverse opinion:** States that the financial statements do not fairly present the company's financial condition
- **Disclaimer of opinion:** Indicates that the auditor has no opinion on the financial statements

Source: Adapted from *AICPA Professional Standards, v. 1, U.S. Auditing Standards, Attestation Standards* (New York: American Institute of Certified Public Accountants, 1995), 654–55.

Canada

- **Standard audit opinion:** Indicates that the financial statements present fairly, in all material respects, the financial position, results of operations, and changes in financial position of the entity in accordance with GAAP

Non-standard auditor's reports:

- **Qualified opinion:** Complies with requirements of standard audit opinion except in specified area referred to in the report
- **Adverse opinion:** States that the financial statements do not fairly present the company's financial condition
- **Denial of opinion:** Indicates that the external auditor is unable to provide an audit opinion

Source: *Reports Prepared by Chartered Accountants—What Do They Mean?* (Toronto: Chartered Accountants of Canada), 3–4.

Current accounting and auditing literature identifies three major types of audits: (1) financial audits, (2) compliance audits, and (3) performance audits. All three types of audits can be conducted on either an internal or external basis. We have discussed financial audits throughout this chapter. Figure 4-8 describes compliance audits and performance audits.

FIGURE 4-8. Compliance Audits and Performance Audits.

Compliance Audit	A ***compliance audit*** verifies that an insurer's financial statements adhere to the laws, regulations, policies, and procedures prescribed by internal or external regulatory authorities. Compliance auditing has been expanded to focus on the market conduct of an insurer's agents. External auditors in the United States use the AICPA's *Compliance Attestation* as a guideline in conducting compliance audits. Insurers in Canada refer to the *CICA Handbook* section on compliance auditing. Tax authorities in the United States and Canada also conduct compliance audits to determine whether an insurer has followed correctly the instructions for completing the federal income tax return and has paid the correct amount of tax.
Performance Audit	A ***performance audit*** measures and evaluates progress toward achieving management objectives for a particular function or goal. A performance audit typically contains an explanation of the processes uncovered in the audit and a report of the auditor's findings and recommendations for improvement. Performance audits require more subjective judgment than financial audits or compliance audits because the purpose of a performance audit is to measure departmental efficiency or effectiveness, rather than adherence to an established set of accounting principles. Two types of performance audits are common. A ***management audit*** focuses on improving the effectiveness and efficiency of an insurer's operations. A ***program results audit*** determines whether the desired results or benefits are actually being achieved under a specified program.

Key Terms and Concepts

internal control
financial auditing
audit
administrative controls
accounting controls
detective control
preventive control
segregation of duties
incompatible functions
fidelity bond
execution of transactions as authorized
authorization level
recording of transactions as executed
safeguarding of assets
physical comparison of recorded amounts
inventory
internal audit
external audit
fraud
collusion
audit trail
auditor's opinion
unqualified opinion
modified opinion
qualified opinion
adverse opinion
disclaimer (denial) of opinion
standard audit opinion
compliance audit
performance audit
management audit
program results audit

Chapter 5

Responsibility Accounting

Chapter Outline

The Role of Management Accounting

Responsibility Accounting
- Responsibility Centers
- Responsibility Center Costs

Performance Measurement and Evaluation
- Variance Analysis
- Responsibility Reports
- Segment Reports

Performance Evaluation Issues
- Cost Allocation
- Revenue Allocation
- Transfer Pricing

OBJECTIVES

After reading this chapter, you should be able to

- Define *responsibility accounting* and identify the distinguishing features of a cost center, profit center, and investment center
- Describe how variance analysis is applied in responsibility centers
- Compare the performance of different profit centers using segment reporting
- Describe the ways that life insurance companies allocate investment income to the investment centers that earn income

Chapter 5 introduces you to the basic concepts of responsibility accounting as they apply to insurance companies. Management decisions, which are based in large part on the insurer's accounting information, directly influence the insurer's financial condition and performance. We begin this chapter with a brief discussion of management functions and the role of management accounting. We then discuss responsibility accounting, the performance measurement and evaluation of responsibility centers, cost allocation, and revenue allocation.

The Role of Management Accounting

Management is a process of actions undertaken to accomplish a stated goal, such as providing a service, making a profit, or achieving a desired rate of return. Managers make hundreds of major and minor decisions about what products and services to sell, whom to hire, what amount to charge customers, how to motivate employees, and so on. In this context, we identify four core management functions—(1) planning, (2) organizing, (3) controlling, and (4) leading—that contribute to informed decision making. ***Decision making***, the process of identifying and selecting a course of action to solve a problem or take advantage of an opportunity, is a critical component of each management function.

The relationships among management functions are circular, rather than linear, as shown in Figure 5-1. For example, the performance standards that are used during the controlling function were established during the planning and organizing functions and used to motivate employees during the leading function. Although a detailed discussion of each management function is beyond the scope of this text, the planning and organizing functions of management directly influence responsibility accounting. A detailed discussion of management functions is covered in FLMI 330: Management Principles and Practices.

Generally, a company's planning activities can be divided into (1) strategic planning, (2) functional-area planning, and (3) operational planning. ***Strategic planning***, sometimes called *corporate planning*, is the process of determining how to pursue comprehensive, organization-wide, long-term goals with available resources. Strategic planning is primarily concerned with long-term projects and activities—typically, two to five years—although the actual period varies among companies. ***Functional-area planning*** is the process of creating long-term plans for various functional areas of a company. ***Operational planning*** is the

FIGURE 5-1. The Relationships Among Management Functions.

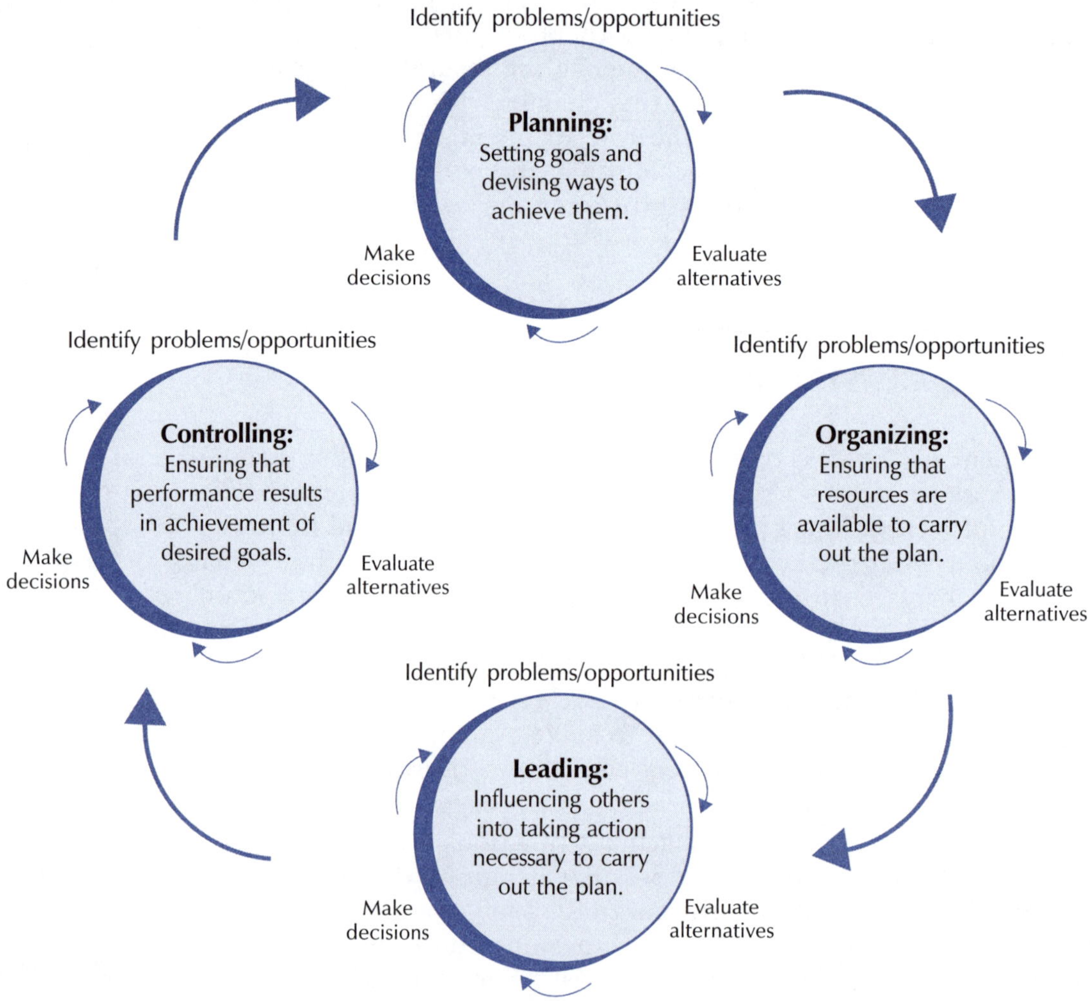

process of determining how to accomplish specified tasks with available resources, given a company's strategic plan. Operational planning is primarily concerned with the short-term, day-to-day activities of a company.

Recall from Chapter 1 that management accounting is the process of identifying, measuring, analyzing, and communicating financial information, so that a company's managers can make informed decisions about the acquisition and use of the company's resources. In Figure 5-2, we examine the individual components of management accounting and an insurance company example of each component. Next, we discuss responsibility accounting.

FIGURE 5-2. Components of the Management Accounting Process.

ACTIVITY	EXAMPLE
Identifying financial information relevant to the decision-making process	Reporting premium income received, by line of business, during a specified accounting period
Measuring the numeric value of things or events	Calculating net income by product line
Analyzing financial information to determine the nature and tendencies associated with the subject being analyzed	Estimating the expected profit margin on permanent life insurance products
Communicating financial information, management's decision, and the reasons for that decision	Distributing periodic reports to managers comparing actual amounts with budgeted amounts.

Responsibility Accounting

A key activity of the organizing function of management is assigning responsibility for specified operations to individuals in the company. In the terminology of management, *responsibility* is an employee's obligation to perform assigned duties. A company should be organized to enable its employees to understand clearly their areas of responsibility. ***Responsibility accounting*** is a people-oriented system of policies and procedures that allows for revenues, expenses, and investments to be assigned to the specified employee or organizational level that is accountable for those specific revenues, expenses, and investments.

Companies use responsibility accounting to prepare and monitor company budgets and to analyze both organization-wide and individual performance. Through responsibility accounting, a company uses its financial information to report internally on the status of operations and other specified areas of management responsibility. By assigning responsibility to specific employees, a company has an effective tool for controlling revenues and expenses, as well as an objective means of evaluating its managers and supervisors.

Responsibility Centers

The area, function, or organizational unit that a specified manager controls is called a ***responsibility center***. The manager of the responsibility center is evaluated according to the performance of the responsibility center. A responsibility center defines the sphere of its manager's responsibility. Under responsibility accounting, responsibility managers should be held accountable only for the revenues, expenses, and investments over which they have direct control. In other words, only those items—such as revenues, costs (expenses), and investments—that can be directly attributable to a given responsibility center are the responsibility of that center's manager.

A responsibility center can be a department, division, line of business, or any other business segment. Figure 5-3 describes several types of responsibility centers. Figure 5-4 shows an example of the organization of responsibility centers in a life insurance company. In this example, we assume that the managers of the individual insurance division have control over capital investment decisions for the division.

FIGURE 5-3. Cost Centers, Profit Centers, and Investment Centers.

In many companies, the distinction among profit centers, cost centers, and investment centers is sometimes blurred. For example, some companies use the term *profit center* to refer to both profit centers and investment centers.

Cost Center

A ***cost center*** is a department or other business segment to which costs (expenses) can be traced. Cost centers do not directly generate revenues or control the assets used to earn profits. Thus, a responsibility manager's main objective in a cost center is to minimize costs while maintaining effective, efficient operations. Examples of insurance company cost centers include the accounting department, legal department, and claims department.

Profit Center

A ***profit center*** is a department or other business segment to which both costs (expenses) and revenues can be traced. Although the responsibility manager of a profit center has direct control over both revenues and expenses associated with the center, the manager does not have direct control over the insurer's assets that are invested in the center. Examples of insurance company profit centers include lines of business—ordinary life insurance, group life insurance, and annuities.

Investment Center

An ***investment center*** is a department or other business segment to which costs (expenses), revenues, and capital or investment funds can be traced. The responsibility manager of an investment center has direct control over the revenues, expenses, and investment funds associated with the center. Examples of an insurer's investment centers include lines of business.

FIGURE 5-4. Organization of Responsibility Centers in an Insurance Company.

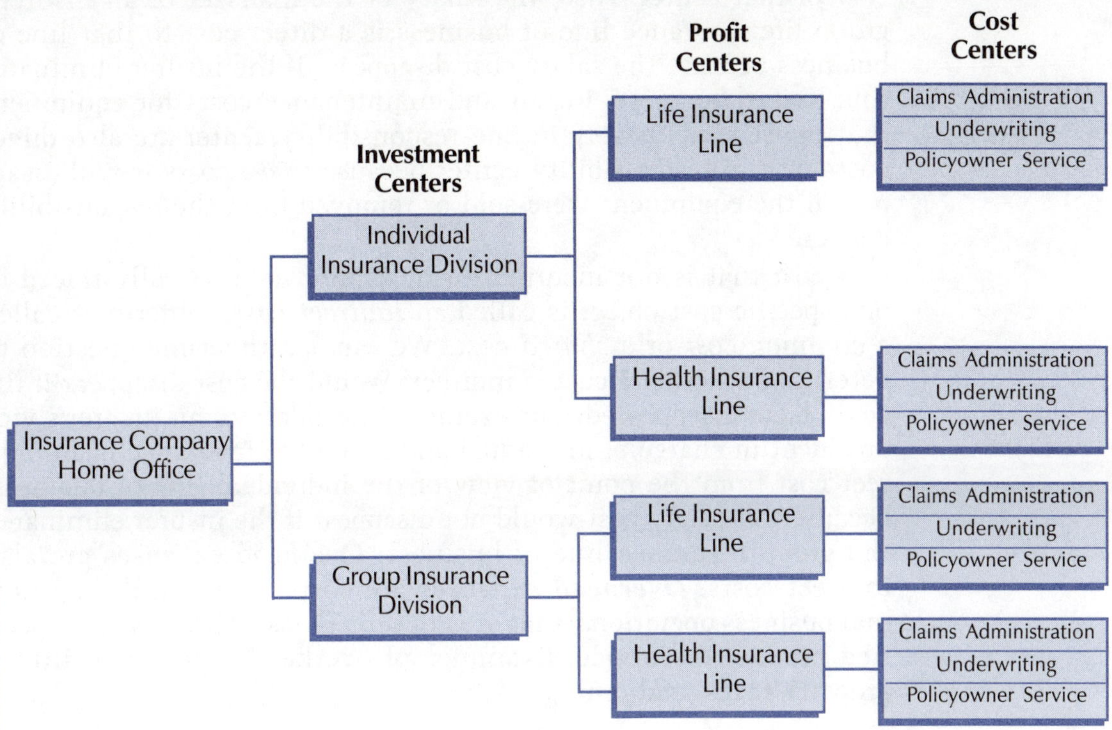

Responsibility Center Costs

To establish and evaluate distinct responsibility centers, a company must be able to separate a center's expenses into categories: (1) controllable and noncontrollable costs and (2) direct and indirect costs. A ***controllable cost*** is a cost over which a responsibility manager has decision-making authority. For example, the costs of supplies, travel, and overtime pay within a department are controllable costs because the department's manager can decide whether or not these costs should be incurred. On the other hand, a ***noncontrollable cost*** is a cost over which a responsibility manager has no decision-making authority. One example of a noncontrollable cost is office rent because a responsibility manager cannot control the rent paid or the portion of the rent allocated to his or her department.

A ***direct cost*** is incurred for or physically traceable to one specific product, line of business, department, or other cost object. A

cost object is any purpose for which a company measures costs. A simple way to determine whether a cost is a direct cost of a specified cost object is to decide whether the cost would disappear if the cost object disappeared. If the answer is yes, then the cost is a direct cost. For example, the salary of a responsibility manager is a direct cost of that center. Also, the salary of the manager of an insurer's group life insurance line of business is a direct cost to that line of business because the salary cost disappears if the insurer eliminates this line of business. Repair and maintenance costs for equipment that is used exclusively in one responsibility center are also direct costs of that responsibility center because these costs would disappear if the equipment were sold or removed from the responsibility center.

A cost that is not incurred for or cannot be physically traced to one specific cost object is called an ***indirect cost***, sometimes called a *common cost* or a *shared cost.* We can ask the same question to determine whether a cost is indirect: Would the cost disappear if the cost object disappeared? For example, the salary of an insurer's vice president in charge of individual and group life insurance is an indirect cost from the point of view of the individual line of business, because this salary cost would not disappear if the insurer eliminated the group insurance line of business. Overhead expenses are also indirect costs. ***Overhead expenses*** are costs, incurred during normal business operations, that are not directly associated with a specified product or service. Examples of overhead costs are utilities, property taxes, and rent.

Performance Measurement and Evaluation

Performance measurement and evaluation are parts of the controlling function of management. Measuring performance involves quantifying the responsibility center's results. Evaluating performance involves assessing the responsibility center's results. Responsibility accounting requires establishing procedures for fairly and accurately measuring and evaluating the performance of responsibility centers and responsibility managers. One technique applicable to all responsibility centers is variance analysis.

Variance Analysis

Whenever an actual result differs from an assumed or expected result, that difference is called a ***variance***. A report that lists variances is an example of a feedback mechanism that informs management to what extent the company's goals are being achieved. ***Variance analysis*** is the study of the difference between expected or assumed results and actual results. Variance analysis is helpful in monitoring and evaluating performance because variances quantify the unexpected results for which responsibility managers are accountable.

Management by exception (MBE) is a principle which states that managers should be informed about operational progress only when a result or activity differs by a specified monetary amount or percentage from what was expected. Management by exception encompasses variance analysis because responsibility managers are alerted only when results or activities differ by a specified amount or percentage from expected results. Large variances are of particular concern to a company's senior managers, who may authorize the development of revised budgets or operational changes.

To be effective, variance analysis must focus on matters that require management attention. Budgets are often used to pinpoint variances from a standard or expected result. Specifically, variance analysis directs a responsibility manager's attention to the differences between budgeted and actual revenues and expenses. For example, if the amount budgeted for the purchase of office equipment is $10,000, and the equipment's actual cost is $12,000, then the variance is $2,000 over budget for that item.

Although variance analysis usually involves studying budgeted and actual results, managers can also use variance analysis to compare other data. For example, a marketing manager may compare the number of new policies written during the current three-month accounting period with the number of new policies written during the previous three-month period or during the same three-month period one year prior. Variance analysis can also compare actual costs with standard costs. We discuss standard costs in Chapter 6.

Rate Variances and Usage Variances

We can categorize variances as either rate variances or usage variances. A product's ***rate variance*** is the difference between the product's actual rate (or unit cost or price) and the rate budgeted for that product, multiplied by the actual number of units sold or processed. A product's ***usage variance*** is the difference between the actual quantities to be sold or processed and the budgeted quantities sold or processed, multiplied by the budgeted rate. The sum of the two variances equals the product's total variance. Figure 5-5 shows how variance analysis can be applied to review claims processing costs.

FIGURE 5-5. Variance Analysis and Claims Processing Costs.

The budget for the claims department of the Ingenuity Life Insurance Company includes the following information on the cost of claims processing:

Actual rate (unit cost per claim)			$ 42
Actual usage (number of claims)			x 1,300
		(a)	$54,600
Budgeted rate			$ 40
Actual usage			x 1,300
		(b)	$52,000
Budgeted rate			$ 40
Budgeted usage			x 1,200
		(c)	$48,000
Rate variance	(a – b)	$2,600	Unfavorable
Usage variance	(b – c)	+ 4,000	Unfavorable
Total variance		$6,600	Unfavorable

Here, Ingenuity's actual results show that its claims department cost center processed 1,300 claims at a total cost of $54,600. The total variance between budgeted costs and actual costs is $6,600 ($54,600 – $48,000). Both the rate and usage components of the total variance are highlighted. Alternately, you could obtain the $2,600 rate variance by subtracting the budgeted rate for the actual rate ($42 – $40), then multiplying the result by 1,300 (the number of actual claims processed).

This variance analysis indicates that the rate variance was unfavorable because Ingenuity's cost of doing business was $2 higher per claim than expected. For this product, the result is both an unfavorable rate variance and an unfavorable usage variance, which leads to an unfavorable total variance of $6,600. In other words, this cost center spent more money to process claims than it had budgeted. Note, however, that the claims processing center processed more claims than Ingenuity expected during the given time period, which resulted in an increase in productivity.

Positive Variances and Negative Variances

Generally, a ***positive variance*** is one in which the actual amount or percentage of an amount is greater than expected, and it is considered favorable for revenue items because, in this case, revenues are higher than expected. Conversely, positive variances are unfavorable for expense items, because they mean that a responsibility center incurred expenses that are higher than expected. Our earlier example of office equipment being over budget is an example of an unfavorable variance. A ***negative variance*** is a variance in which the actual amount or percentage is less than expected, which is favorable for expense items and unfavorable for revenue items. Keep in mind that a positive variance is not identical to a favorable variance. Similarly, a negative variance is not necessarily an unfavorable variance. We discuss favorable and unfavorable variances in the context of standard costs in Chapter 6.

Responsibility Reports

A ***responsibility report***, sometimes called a *responsibility center report*, is a management accounting report that itemizes budgeted and actual amounts that are under the responsibility manager's sphere of control and the corresponding variance for each revenue or cost (expense). Items that a responsibility manager cannot control are either omitted from the responsibility report or are listed separately.

Figure 5-6 highlights the policyowner service function on the organizational chart of the Emerald Life Insurance Company. Figure 5-7 describes and shows the monthly responsibility reports for Emerald's policyowner service centers at three different levels.

Segment Reports

The evaluation of a profit center should be based on the profits earned by the center. One way to monitor profit centers is to prepare a specific responsibility report, sometimes called a segment report. A ***segment report*** is a type of management accounting report that shows revenues and expenses for a single responsibility center. Segment reports for profit centers generally take the form of an income statement because these reports show both revenues and expenses.

Although segment reporting is primarily a management accounting tool, segment reports are sometimes required for financial reporting purposes. For example, the *Analysis of Operations by Lines of Business* exhibit in the U.S. Annual Statement is an example of a segment report. Also, the GAAP-based annual report of a large U.S. company must include revenues and profits for each significant business segment of the company.

A profit center's segment report details activity at each management level, including condensed information from operations that are subordinate to the managerial level. Thus, as we move downward from one level to the next, we examine a smaller portion of the company. Segment reports separate direct and indirect costs at each management level, and also include revenues.

FIGURE 5-6. Organization of Policyowner Service Function Responsibilities.

Emerald's senior vice president of policyowner service is responsible for both the East and West divisions of the policyowner service function. The assistant vice president in charge of each division is responsible for five departments in that division. Each policyowner service department has a responsibility manager who is directly responsible for the department.

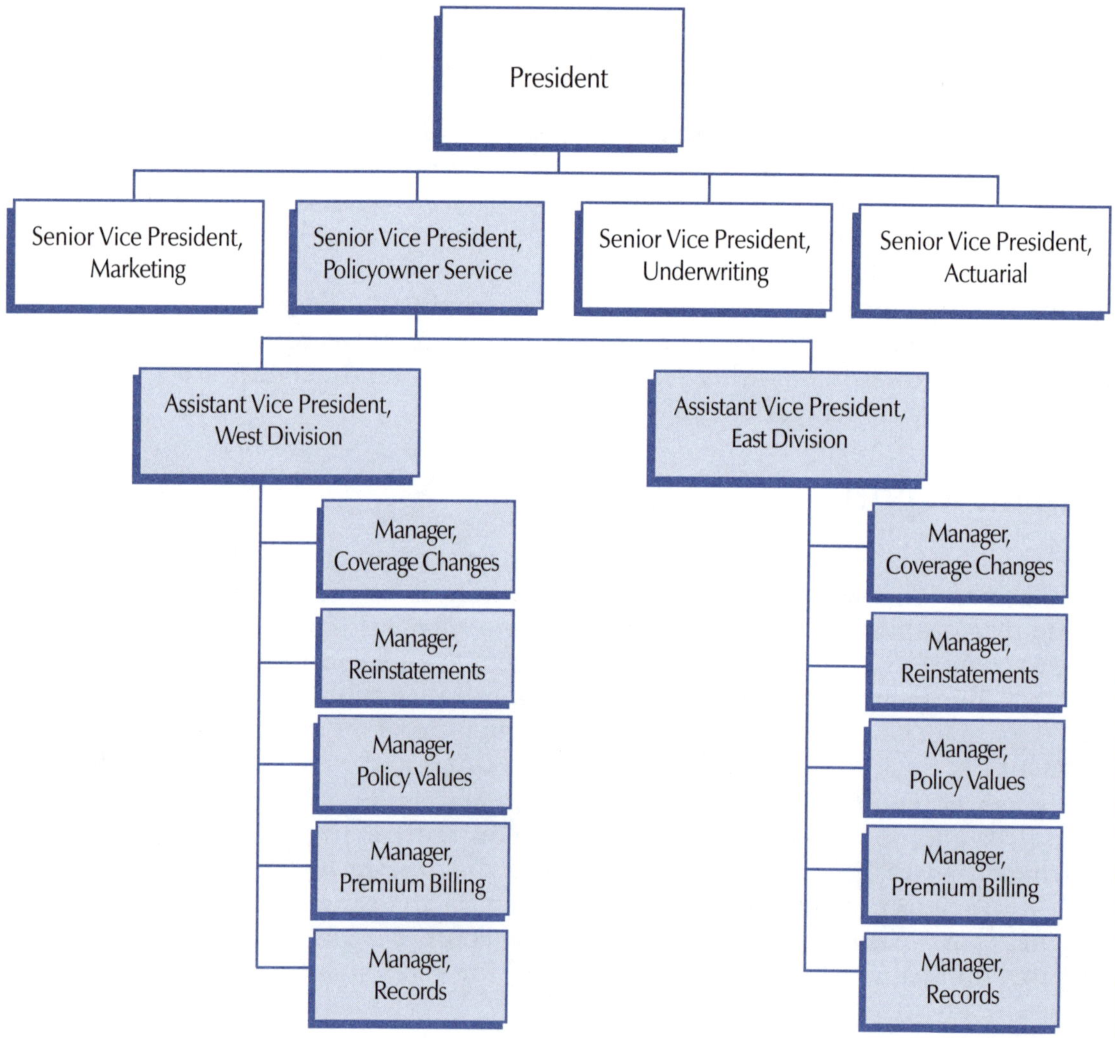

Performance Evaluation Issues

In practice, achieving an accurate summary of performance is rarely so straightforward as preparing a report or calculating a ratio. For

FIGURE 5-7. Policyowner Service Responsibility Reports.

Policyowner service is a cost center; therefore, its responsibility report includes only costs. The responsibility report for each organizational level includes the costs of each responsibility center below it. For example, the responsibility report for the West division's reinstatements department includes $13,800 budgeted for salaries and bonuses. This amount is also included in the $30,435 budgeted total on the "Reinstatements" line of the responsibility report for the assistant vice president of the West division of policyowner service. Further, this amount is included on the "West Division" line of the responsibility report for the senior vice president of policyowner service.

The example shows how responsibility reports can serve (1) to assist senior management in controlling responsibility center performance and (2) to enable each responsibility manager to uncover information about the center's operations, including clues for improving cost control during the next accounting period.

Note that the report for each management level includes both direct and indirect costs. As the segments become more narrowly defined, direct and indirect costs are allocated accordingly. However, as one responsibility report is divided into smaller segmented reports, certain direct fixed costs from the larger segment may become indirect fixed costs on a smaller segment. As a result, total costs attributable to one manager are greater than the sum of the direct costs attributable to each individual department under that manager's supervision.

For example, the responsibility report for the assistant vice president, West division, includes the direct costs incurred by the division's five departments and the $16,000 budgeted costs that are common to the five departments. A portion of this $16,000 could be the assistant vice president's salary. This point emphasizes the concept of controllable costs under responsibility accounting because the assistant vice president's salary is not under the control of any of the five departments. Rather, this salary is under the control of the senior vice president, policyowner service.

Senior Vice President, Policyowner Service		**($000s)**	
	Actual	**Budget**	**Variance**
Direct divisional costs:			
West Division	$153,621	$153,935	$ 314
East Division	135,227	138,900	3,673
Total direct costs	$288,848	$292,835	$ 3,987
Indirect costs to divisions	90,213	87,450	(2,763)
Total costs	$379,061	$380,285	$ 1,224

Assistant Vice President, West Division	**Actual**	**Budget**	**Variance**
Direct departmental costs:			
Coverage changes	$ 31,622	$ 33,425	$ 1,803
Reinstatements	34,530	30,435	(4,095)
Policy values	21,845	20,950	(895)
Premium billing	23,338	24,575	1,237
Records	26,436	28,550	2,114
Total direct costs	$137,771	$137,935	$ 164
Indirect costs to departments	15,850	16,000	150
Total costs	$153,621	$153,935	$ 314

Manager, West Division Reinstatements	**Actual**	**Budget**	**Variance**
Direct costs:			
Salaries and bonuses	$14,250	$13,800	$ (450)
Office supplies	195	235	40
Toll-free phone lines	10,037	6,000	(4,037)
Policyowner service training	2,825	2,900	75
Total direct costs	$27,307	$22,935	$ (4,372)
Indirect costs	7,223	7,500	277
Total costs	$34,530	$30,435	$ (4,095)

example, a premise of responsibility accounting is that responsibility managers should be held accountable for only the costs that they directly control. But few costs are clearly the responsibility of only one manager. Most costs have varying degrees of controllability.

The purpose of responsibility management is to identify the manager most directly responsible for incurring each cost. Several related issues must also be considered in the evaluation process. Some issues are problems inherent in the evaluation process itself. Other issues may affect a responsibility center's performance and, if not considered, may lead to an inaccurate assessment of the center. Thus, the evaluation criteria can be as important as the actual performance in the evaluation process. Insight 5-1 describes potential problems with performance evaluation criteria. The following section discusses factors that can influence the performance evaluation of a responsibility center.

Insight 5-1. Problems with Evaluative Criteria.

Overemphasis on Variance Analysis

Isolating budget variances is a common method for evaluating a responsibility center's performance. The exclusive use of variance analysis can be misleading, because senior management has a tendency to focus on variances that negatively affect a responsibility center. However, variances that appear to positively affect a responsibility center should also be scrutinized. For example, a dramatic increase in new business that might appear to benefit the insurer may be the result of using lax underwriting standards that could result in extensive losses to the insurer at a later date.

Use of a Single Evaluation Criterion

Another evaluation problem occurs when a company's senior management focuses a responsibility manager's performance evaluation on one goal and ignores all other company goals. Suppose an insurer's underwriters are evaluated solely on the number of policies they approve. If the insurer bases the job stability and promotions of its underwriters on this one criterion, then underwriters may be tempted to approve every policy application. Eventually, the insurer would lose money from paying out so many claims. Therefore, the insurer evaluates the performance of its underwriters on additional criteria.

Use of Inappropriate Criteria

Performance criteria that fails to measure the results of a responsibility center against a company's goals is ineffective. Nonetheless, some companies focus management evaluations on short-term results. Responsibility managers in such cases may be tempted to forsake long-term company goals and overuse current resources to maximize their short-term results in order to earn a satisfactory performance evaluation. The long-term consequences may include insufficient resources to achieve future company goals.

Unattainable Goals

Evaluation problems can arise when performance standards are not attainable by responsibility managers. For example, a responsibility manager may be evaluated unfavorably for failing to achieve goals that are unrealistic. Senior management can avoid this problem by becoming aware of how the budgets and other standards are determined and to what extent controllability is considered in the comparison of budgeted and actual results. Also, a company can involve its responsibility managers in budget preparation.

Responsibility Managers versus Responsibility Centers

Senior management evaluates responsibility managers apart from their responsibility centers. A responsibility manager's performance may be good, even though the responsibility center's performance is poor. This situation can happen to the responsibility manager of a business segment in a declining market. Conversely, a business segment in a growing market may be thriving, but not as a result of the responsibility manager's accomplishments. Then senior management can determine whether the manager's performance has affected the center's performance or whether the center's performance was primarily a function of its environment.

Cost Allocation

Cost allocation is the accounting process of assigning or distributing an indirect cost (expense) according to a specified method or formula. Cost allocation is somewhat arbitrary because internal influences, insufficient data to properly allocate costs, or a flawed allocation method or formula can result in improper or unfair cost allocations. Keep in mind that the choice of method used for cost allocation, and the selection of allocation bases for each method, will affect the results of an insurer's responsibility centers and their managers. We discuss cost allocation methods in Chapter 6.

Revenue Allocation

So far our discussion has focused on the importance of appropriately allocating costs to responsibility centers. However, unless a company accurately allocates its revenues to the responsibility centers that are accountable for those revenues, the performance of the company's responsibility centers and managers cannot be fairly measured and evaluated. If a responsibility center's revenues are overstated or understated, management decisions about the center can be impaired.

Recall that the primary sources of revenues for life insurance companies are (1) premium income from the sale of insurance policies and annuities, (2) investment income from earnings on the insurer's assets, and (3) fee income from providing various administrative services. Allocating premium income and fee income to the appropriate responsibility center is generally straightforward because income items are typically identified by product type, such as term life insurance or variable annuities. But allocating investment income to particular products or lines of business is more difficult than allocating premium income or fee income. Insight 5-2 summarizes several common methods that life insurance companies use to allocate investment income to responsibility centers.

Transfer Pricing

Evaluating the performance of specific responsibility centers such as profit centers and investment centers can be more challenging when transfer pricing is involved. A ***transfer price*** is the price of a good or service that one business segment or line of business charges another segment or line of the same company. For example, the human resources department of an insurer may use transfer pricing to charge the insurer's group life insurance line of business for employee recruitment or training expenses. Unlike intercompany transactions, in which prices are determined by market factors such as supply and demand, transfer pricing arrangements are intracompany in nature—that is, they are established by a company's internal

Insight 5-2. Investment Income Allocation Methods.

Mean Liabilities Method

The ***mean liabilities method*** allocates investment income to lines of business on the basis of the reserves that are attributable to each line. For example, if 40 percent of an insurer's reserves are attributable to group life insurance, then the responsibility center that is accountable for group life insurance is allocated 40 percent of the insurer's investment income.

One problem associated with the use of the mean liabilities method is that newer lines of business may be allocated a share of the investment income generated by older, high-yielding investments that were purchased before the new products existed. Also, the mean liabilities method does not consider the impact of the surplus required to support a line of business.

Investment Year Method

The ***investment year method*** forms separate investment pools that contain the investments made during each year, thus overcoming one weakness of the mean liabilities method. Under the investment year method, a share of the investment pool for each calendar year is in turn allocated to each product line or line of business. Each line's share of investment income is determined by the investable funds generated by that line each year. ***Investable funds*** consist of (1) net income before taxes, (2) investment income received on prior investments, and (3) the maturities of principal on prior investments.

Under the investment year method, an insurer's newer product lines—which have lower amounts of accumulated funds and larger cash outflows from current operations—receive relatively larger shares of investment income from newer investments. The insurer's older lines of business—which typically have larger reserves and lower amounts of cash outflows—receive larger shares of investment income from older investments.

Investment Segmentation Method

In the ***investment segmentation method***, an insurer uses the cash flows of a product line or line of business to purchase specific investments for that line. In essence, the insurer treats each product line as though the product line owned specified investments. The investment income from each investment is in turn allocated to the line that acquired the investment.

Under the investment segmentation method, separate investment strategies can be developed for different product lines. This versatility is important because cash flow patterns and the investment income requirements differ among product lines. For example, the cash flows of an insurer's annuity business differ from those of its ordinary life insurance business.

The method used depends in part on the insurer's objectives. If an insurer's primary goal of selecting an allocation method is to comply with statutory requirements for completing the U.S. Annual Statement, then the mean liabilities method is adequate. On the other hand, if the insurer also wants to accurately evaluate its responsibility centers, then the insurer would most likely use the investment year method or the investment segmentation method.

management team. Transfer pricing is especially important for insurance companies that have subsidiaries or are themselves subsidiaries.

The transfer pricing method that an insurer selects is critical, because transfer prices directly affect the profits for which the responsibility managers of profit centers and investment centers are held accountable. An inappropriate transfer price might result in a misleading evaluation of a responsibility center's performance. Moreover, inappropriate transfer prices may lead a responsibility manager to make decisions that are not in the insurer's best interest. A discussion of the process of setting transfer prices is beyond the scope of this text.

Key Terms and Concepts

decision making
strategic planning
functional-area planning
operational planning
responsibility accounting
responsibility center
cost center
profit center
investment center
controllable cost
noncontrollable cost
direct cost
cost object
indirect cost
overhead expenses
variance
variance analysis
management by exception (MBE)
rate variance
usage variance
positive variance
negative variance
responsibility report
segment report
cost allocation
mean liabilities method
investment year method
investable funds
investment segmentation method
transfer price

Chapter 6

Cost Accounting

Chapter Outline

Cost Classification
- Descriptive Classification
- Classification by Behavior
- Classification by Measurement
- Cost Perspectives

Cost Accumulation
- Accumulating Costs by Type
- Accumulating Costs by Line of Business
- Accumulating Costs by Department or Cost Center
- Accumulating Costs by Function
- Cost Perspectives

Allocation Bases
- Indirect Salaries
- Indirect Expenses Other Than Salaries

OBJECTIVES

After reading this chapter, you should be able to

- Recognize the primary uses of cost accounting in life insurance companies
- Identify and distinguish costs that are classified by description, behavior, and measurement
- Interpret how costs are accumulated by type, by line of business, by cost center, and by function
- Recognize the basic methods of service department cost allocation

Chapter 6 discusses cost classification and describes the methods that companies use to allocate, analyze, and control costs. Cost control is a management accounting subject of considerable interest to life insurance companies. To support their cost control programs, insurers employ cost accounting systems. ***Cost accounting*** is a system for accumulating expense data used to facilitate effective cost control and accurate estimates of future costs for use in the pricing of a company's products. A cost accounting system is used to define, describe, accumulate, record, and assign all the costs incurred by a company. Figure 6-1 presents several common insurance applications of cost accounting.

Generally, companies have the freedom to design cost accounting systems that satisfy their unique needs. As a result, cost accounting systems vary greatly among companies, and possibly even among different divisions of the same company. A critical element of an effective cost accounting system is identifying costs by product line, line of business, division, and/or function. As cost identification becomes more specific, the overall effectiveness of a company's cost accounting system increases.

Cost Classification

Insurers first classify costs in practical ways so the insurer's cost accounting system produces useful management reports. The definition

FIGURE 6-1. Insurance Applications of Cost Accounting.

- Determine the costs of creating, marketing, and servicing products so they are priced appropriately
- Match the costs incurred during a given accounting period to the income earned in or attributed to that same period
- Determine the costs incurred during a given accounting period by product type, line of business, or by subsidiary or affiliated company

- Provide managers with useful information for analyzing problems in functional areas
- Budget resources to support various strategic goals
- Determine policy dividend scales
- Evaluate the efficiency of corporate procedures and personnel

ascribed to a cost classification reflects both the attributes of the cost and the circumstances surrounding the cost. Costs are typically classified by (1) description, (2) behavior, and (3) measurement. Keep in mind that many of these costs have similar or shared characteristics. Where appropriate, we describe shared characteristics.

Descriptive Classification

The most common way to classify costs is by their descriptive characteristics. Figure 6-2 presents definitions and examples of cost classification by description. Recall that Chapter 5 discussed direct and indirect costs and controllable and noncontrollable costs.

FIGURE 6-2. Cost Classification by Description.

Cost Classification	Definition	Example
Direct cost	A cost that is physically traceable to a single cost object	To the group life insurance line of business, the salary of the division manager of group life insurance
Indirect cost	A cost that is not physically traceable to a single cost object	To the group life insurance line of business, the salary of the vice president in charge of all group insurance
Controllable cost	A cost over which a responsibility manager has decision making authority	To a line of business, the cost of its supplies, travel, and employee overtime
Noncontrollable cost	A cost over which a responsibility manager has no decision making authority	To a line of business, home office rent and depreciation on equipment
Differential cost	A cost that changes as a result of a future decision	To the group insurance division, costs that are incurred only if a line of business is added to the division
Sunk cost	A cost that does not change as a result of a future decision	To a line of business, existing salary costs that will not change as a result of the decision to undertake a specified project
Committed cost	A cost that results from a prior management decision and that cannot be changed quickly	To a life insurer, the costs of existing facilities, equipment, systems development, and executive salaries
Discretionary cost	A cost that results from periodic management decisions that change as conditions change	To a life insurer, the costs of product advertising, promotional campaigns, and employee training

Classification by Behavior

Time and volume are the defining factors when classifying costs by behavior. Some costs change as the amount of time needed to complete an activity changes. Other costs change as the volume of activity changes. Many costs change with both time and volume, and some costs are not affected by time or volume at all. As shown in Figure 6-3, costs that can be defined by behavior are most commonly classified as (1) fixed costs, (2) variable costs, and (3) semi-variable costs.

Classification by Measurement

Costs classified by measurement are especially helpful for management reports and for cost-volume-profit analysis, which we describe in Chapter 7. Costs classified by measurement include (1) unit costs, (2) standard costs, (3) marginal costs, (4) marginal unit costs, and (5) opportunity costs.

Unit Costs

Unit costs are a basic measurement in cost accounting. A ***unit cost*** is the incurred expense attributable to a single measured amount of work. Both fixed costs and variable costs can be expressed in terms of unit costs. To find the unit cost, divide the total costs by the number of units. Normally, as production volume or the amount of activity increases, fixed unit costs decrease. As volume decreases, fixed unit costs increase. Examples of unit costs are cost per

- Policy issued
- $1,000 of insurance coverage (face amount) issued
- $100 of agent commissions paid
- $1,000 of investment income

Suppose an insurance company sold 400,000 policies in 2000 and 500,000 policies in 2001. Assume that the company's total fixed costs in each year are $8,000,000. As shown in the following table, fixed unit costs generally decrease as volume increases.

Year	2000	2001
Policies sold	400,000	500,000
Total fixed costs	$8,000,000	$8,000,000
Unit fixed costs	$20	$16

FIGURE 6-3. Characteristics of Fixed Costs, Variable Costs, and Semi-Variable Costs.

FIXED COSTS

A ***fixed cost*** is a cost that remains constant for all levels of operating activity or production. Examples of an insurer's fixed costs are rent for a branch office and fire insurance for the home office facility. Whether an insurance company sells or services one policy or one million policies during a given period, these fixed costs remain the same. We can further classify fixed costs as either committed costs or discretionary costs, which we described earlier.

VARIABLE COSTS

The amount of a ***variable cost*** changes in direct response to changes in the level of operating activity. An example of a variable cost is agent commissions. If an insurer sells no insurance policies, there are no agent commission costs. However, as sales volume increases, the cost of commissions also increases. Another variable cost is the cost of premium processing. The higher the sales volume, the more premium processing costs the insurer incurs.

SEMI-VARIABLE COSTS

A ***semi-variable cost***, also called a *mixed cost*, contains elements of both fixed costs and variable costs and is comprised of a fixed cost component plus the amount of a variable component over time and at each volume level. Semi-variable costs include electricity, heat, repairs, telephone, and building maintenance costs.

For example, the cost of electricity involves a basic monthly service charge to have electricity available for use. This charge is the fixed cost component, and it remains the same each month regardless of how much electricity the insurer uses. Even when the insurer uses no electricity, there is still a fixed cost for basic service. The variable component of the insurer's electricity cost includes the number of kilowatt-hours of electricity the company uses. If the insurer shuts off all of its office lights every night, it will use fewer kilowatt-hours of electricity—and therefore incur a lower variable electricity cost—than if it keeps its lights on all night.

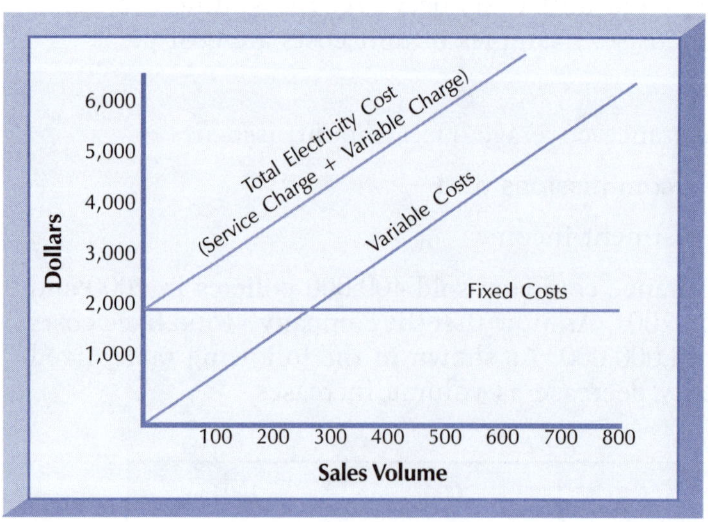

Note that fixed costs remain the same for all levels of sales volume, variable costs increase as the volume of sales increases, and semi-variable costs—such as electricity use—have both a fixed component and a variable component.

Standard Costs

Unit costs are often used to express standard costs. A ***standard cost*** is a predetermined cost expected to be incurred for particular items during normal business operations. Many companies establish a standard cost for each item against which they later compare the actual cost. Two important standard costs for insurance companies are the unit cost of processing one claim and the unit cost of maintaining one policy. An insurer first establishes a standard cost for processing one claim, then compares that standard cost with the actual unit cost of processing a claim. Next, the insurer conducts variance analysis to determine how to better manage costs.

Recall from Chapter 5 that a variance occurs when an actual result differs from an assumed or expected result. In the context of cost accounting, a variance occurs whenever the actual cost differs from the standard cost. Variances may be favorable or unfavorable, depending on the relationship between actual costs and standard costs. A ***favorable variance*** is a variance in which the standard cost is higher than the actual cost. An ***unfavorable variance*** is a variance in which the actual cost is higher than the standard cost.

For example, an insurer establishes a standard cost of $35 to process each claim. If the actual cost to process each claim is $33, then the result is a favorable variance because the $35 standard cost is higher than the $33 actual cost. Suppose the actual cost to process each claim was $38. In this case, the result would be an unfavorable variance, because the $38 actual cost is higher than the $35 standard cost, as shown in the following table.

Quarter	Quarter 1	Quarter 2
Standard cost	$35	$35
Actual cost	$33	$38
Variance	$2 favorable	($3) unfavorable

Marginal Costs

A ***marginal cost***, also called an *incremental cost*, is the additional total expense incurred as a result of producing one additional unit of an existing product or service. Marginal cost information helps managers to determine the monetary effect of a specific action, and, in certain cases, whether an action should or should not be taken. For example, if an agent submits 50 policy applications per year at a total cost of $40,000, and the total cost of processing 51 policy applications is $40,500, then the marginal cost of the 51st application is $500 ($40,500 – $40,000), as shown in the following table. Note that a marginal cost could also be determined for processing the 52nd and 53rd applications, and so on.

Number of Policy Applications	Total Cost	Marginal Cost
50	$40,000	—
51	$40,500	$500

Some costs involved in processing the initial amount may not apply to the additional production. In the previous example, the agent's submission of the 51st application would probably not cost as much as 1/50th of $40,000 ($800), because most of the total expenses—such as advertising, office supplies, and office space—are already committed costs or sunk costs. These costs are thus unaffected by the processing of a single additional application. Alternatively, the additional submission may incur costs, such as overtime pay, that were not required for the initial amount of processing. Keep in mind that the marginal cost of each additional unit is different from the unit cost of the initial amount produced.

Marginal costs are similar to differential costs. In this text, we refer to the additional total expense incurred as a result of producing one additional unit of an existing product or service as a marginal cost. However, a differential cost is incurred as a result of a management decision to undertake a new product or service. After a certain sales volume has been reached, the decision to produce or sell additional units involves different cost considerations (marginal costs) than did the earlier decision to produce or sell the initial amount of a new product or service (differential costs).

Marginal Unit Costs

To help make production decisions, managers consider the ***marginal unit cost***, which is the increase or decrease in the unit cost as a result of an additional unit of a good or service. Figure 6-4 depicts an example of the marginal costs and marginal unit costs incurred in an insurer's policy issue department. This example assumes that departmental salaries do not increase during the period of study.

Opportunity Costs

In making decisions about expenditures, most managers are aware of out-of-pocket costs. An ***out-of-pocket cost*** is a cost that requires

FIGURE 6-4. Marginal Costs and Marginal Unit Costs.

In Year 1, 50 employees issue 20,000 policies. Suppose the department incurs total costs of $7,000,000, including $1,500,000 for employee-related items (such as salaries, employee benefits, workspace, etc.), and $5,500,000 in other expenses (such as supplies, policy forms, and computer run time) in Year 1.

Thus, the Year 1 unit cost per policy issued is $350 ($7,000,000 ÷ 20,000) as seen in column 6. In Year 2, policies issued increases by 300 to 20,300. The department manager believes that the current staff can handle the extra workload. The expected additional costs incurred are $10,000 in other expenses. In this case, the marginal cost for the additional 300 policies is $10,000, and the marginal unit cost per policy for each additional policy is $33.33 ($10,000 ÷ 300). Note that the unit cost per policy for all policies drops from $350 in Year 1 to $345.32 in Year 2.

In Year 3, the department issues an additional 300 policies, bringing the cumulative total that year to 20,600. The department manager believes that more staff will be required to handle this increase, so another employee is added at an employee-related cost of $35,000. In addition, the department incurs $10,000 in other expenses, bringing the total additional costs incurred during Year 3 to $45,000. This $45,000 represents the marginal costs for the newest 300 policies. When the manager faces the situation of processing an additional 300 policies in Year 3, the marginal unit cost per policy for the 300 additional policies jumps to $150 ($45,000 ÷ 300) as a result of hiring an additional employee. The unit cost per policy for all 20,600 policies is $342.48.

	1 Number of Policies Issued	2 Number of Employees	3 Employee-Related Expenses	4 Other Policy Expenses	5 Total Expenses {3} + {4}	6 Unit Cost {5} ÷ {1}
Year 1	20,000 300	50	$1,500,000	$5,500,000 10,000	$7,000,000 10,000 **	$350.00 * $ 33.33 ***
Year 2	20,300 300	50 1	$1,500,000 35,000	$5,510,000 10,000	$7,010,000 45,000 **	$345.32 * $150.00 ***
Year 3	20,600	51	$1,535,000	$5,520,000	$7,055,000	$342.48 *

* Unit cost for each policy
** Marginal cost for additional 300 policies
*** Marginal unit cost for each additional policy

outlays of cash or other resources. However, managers sometimes overlook the opportunity costs associated with a decision. An ***opportunity cost*** is the benefit that is forfeited or given up in choosing one decision alternative over another. Managers must be aware that all out-of-pocket costs carry associated opportunity costs.

Suppose a life insurance company is considering introducing a new universal life product. The company estimates that the out-of-pocket cost of this project will be $1 million for research, actuarial work, systems, and marketing. What are the opportunity costs associated with this project? The company could use the $1 million to enhance its current universal life operating systems. These improved existing systems may provide a return that equals or exceeds the return offered by the new product alone. The company could also use the $1 million to purchase assets to generate investment income.

There is no definitive way to capture opportunity costs in the accounting system because no transaction is involved. Managers should therefore analyze various business scenarios to determine the cost of making each business decision. In the above example, the project manager would make revenue and expense projections associated with (1) undertaking the new product, (2) enhancing the existing operating systems, and (3) investing in income-producing assets.

Cost Perspectives

We have seen that a single cost can be classified in several different ways, depending on the point of view of the person analyzing the cost and the point of view of the department incurring the cost. For example, the salary of an insurer's vice president of marketing is

- A *direct* cost of the marketing division as a whole
- An *indirect* cost with respect to the individual life insurance marketing department within the marketing division
- A *fixed* cost that remains unchanged regardless of the activity of the division
- A *controllable* cost to the chief executive officer of the company
- A *committed* cost that resulted from a prior management decision regarding the operation of the company

Cost Accumulation

Ideally, a cost accounting system should provide responsibility managers with sufficient information to make informed decisions about the operations for which they are accountable. A cost accounting system should accumulate costs and allocate costs accurately and fairly. ***Cost accumulation*** is the process of capturing all company costs and categorizing them in meaningful ways. Four methods of accumulating cost data are by (1) type, (2) line of business, (3) department or cost center, and (4) function. Many insurers accumulate costs by two or more methods in order to determine whether the costs associated with one classification, line of business, department, or function, are greater than or less than expected.

Accumulating Costs by Type

In accumulating costs by type, a company accumulates costs without regard to the specified area of the company that incurs the expense. For example, all company costs relating to salaries can be included in the "Salaries" classification, instead of being itemized by department or line of business. Accumulating costs by type enables companies to satisfy financial reporting requirements. In addition, this method of cost accumulation assists managers in determining which costs are increasing or decreasing over time. However, accumulating costs by type does not explain which areas of the company incur each cost and, therefore, who or what is responsible for changes in cost levels.

Accumulating Costs by Line of Business

When accumulating costs by line of business, all costs that are associated with a particular line are charged to that line. In the context of cost accounting, a ***line of business*** is a segment of products that has a cost pattern distinct from that of other product segments. Examples of an insurer's lines of business include individual life insurance, annuities, and group life insurance. An insurer generally first accumulates costs according to type, then codes the monetary amount or percentage that applies to each line of business, such as annuities or group life insurance.

Accumulating Costs by Department or Cost Center

Another cost accumulation method is by department or cost center. Recall from Chapter 5 that a cost center is a department or other business segment to which costs can be charged. Cost centers typically accumulate their costs according to the various levels of accumulation, such as type and function. When accumulating costs by cost center, the costs of departments at each level of a company are absorbed into the cost reports for departments at higher levels in the organization. This type of cost accumulation enables management to judge the performance of individual cost centers.

Accumulating Costs by Function

When costs are accumulated by function, they are directed to the company operation that generates the costs. A ***function*** consists of a series of activities that serve a specific purpose. For example, policy maintenance is a typical insurance company function, and all the costs associated with the maintenance of in-force policies are typically charged to that function. Activities within the policy maintenance function include collecting renewal premiums, processing agent renewal commissions, administering policy loans, and processing policy surrenders.

The accumulated costs of the activities involved within a certain function, without regard to organizational units, are known as ***functional costs***. Within each function are the costs of salaries, supplies, equipment, and so on. Figure 6-5 shows the accumulation of costs for a specific insurer's policy maintenance function within the individual life insurance line of business. Note that this insurer accumulates functional costs by both line of business and cost center.

Accumulating costs by function is generally more complicated than accumulating costs by type or cost center. Functional cost accumulation involves identifying and measuring all the activities involved in a given function. Some activities may be involved in more than one function. In this case, it is necessary to allot the correct portion of an activity's cost to each function that uses the activity.

Cost Perspectives

Again, we can classify a single cost in different ways. For instance, the cost of underwriting applications for a new term life insurance product is

FIGURE 6-5. Accumulation of Policy Maintenance Costs by Line of Business and Cost Center.

Policy Maintenance Function
Individual Life Insurance
($000s)

	Salary	Benefits	Operations	Overhead	Subtotal
Cost Center 1: Premium Collection	$200	$20	$100	$50	$370
Cost Center 2: Commission Processing	175	35	90	70	370
Cost Center 3: Policyowner Service					
Activity A: Policy Administration	210	25	140	60	435
Activity B: Surrender Administration	100	10	80	30	220
Subtotal	$310	$35	$220	$ 90	$ 655
Total Policy Maintenance Costs	$685	$90	$410	$210	$1,395

- An underwriting cost when accumulated by type
- A term life insurance cost when accumulated by line of business
- An underwriting department cost when accumulated by cost center
- A policy acquisition cost when accumulated by function

Once a company accumulates all costs, it then allocates them to the department, function, and line of business that was responsible for generating them. This process is known as *cost allocation*. In Chapter 5, we briefly discussed cost allocation, which is the accounting process of assigning or distributing an indirect cost according to a method or formula. Through the use of cost allocation methods, a company's managers have a better understanding of the sources of company costs. Figure 6-6 shows how one company allocates the cost of salaries first to cost centers and then to functions by line of business.

FIGURE 6-6. Cost Allocation to Cost Centers and to Functions by Line of Business.

1. *Allocate salary costs to cost centers*

Cost Center	Total Allocations
#1000: Individual Premium Collection	$ 1,000
#2000: Individual Commissions	1,000
#3000: Individual Policyowner Service	1,000
Total Salary Costs	$ 3,000*

2. *Allocate salary costs to functions by line of business*

	Allocations
#1000: Individual Premium Collection	
A. Individual Life New Business	$ 200
B. Individual Health New Business	100
C. Individual Annuities New Business	100
D. Individual Life Policy Maintenance	300
E. Individual Health Policy Maintenance	200
F. Individual Annuities Policy Maintenance	100
Subtotal	$ 1,000
#2000: Individual Commissions	1,000
#3000: Individual Policyowner Service	1,000
Total Salary Costs	$ 3,000*

* Note that this company incurs $3,000 in salary costs, so the total amount it allocates to cost centers and functions is $3,000.

Allocation Bases

To help ensure an equitable allocation of indirect costs, insurers seek an ***allocation base***, or measure of use, that exhibits a proportional relationship between the indirect cost and the cost center being allocated a portion of that cost. Different allocation methods and allocation bases are typically appropriate for various types of costs. Figure 6-7 discusses several common allocation bases.

Indirect Salaries

Salaries usually represent the largest percentage of indirect costs in a life insurance company. The allocation of a divisional vice president's salary to each department in that division must be as precise as possible if the company allocates other expenses in proportion to employee salaries. Most companies allocate indirect salary costs by using ***time analysis***, which determines the percentage of time that each employee spends with different departments or activities. A discussion of time analysis is beyond the scope of this text.

FIGURE 6-7. Common Allocation Bases.

Amount of square footage

Under this allocation base, indirect costs are allocated according to the size of a cost center's workspace. Costs such as utility bills are often allocated to cost centers according to square footage. For example, if one cost center uses 12 percent of an insurer's office space and another uses 8 percent, the total amounts of the insurer's utility bills would be allocated to each cost center according to these percentages.

Number of employees

Under this allocation base, indirect costs are assigned to cost centers according to the relative number of employees in each cost center. For example, a cost center with 63 percent of an insurer's employees would be allocated 63 percent of the insurer's indirect costs. The more employees a cost center requires, the larger its allocated share of indirect costs.

Percentage of direct costs

This allocation base assumes that cost centers should be allocated indirect costs in proportion to the level of direct costs they generate. Suppose an insurer's new business department incurs 17 percent of an insurer's direct costs in a year. In this case, the insurer would allocate 17 percent of all indirect costs to the new business department.

Indirect Expenses Other Than Salaries

Indirect expenses other than salaries include rent, utilities, institutional advertising, association dues, medical fees, and information processing services. A decision whether to distribute non-salary expenses among cost centers depends on several factors, including company size and the level of financial information needed for decision making. Methods of allocating indirect expenses other than salaries are somewhat arbitrary and differ among companies. Typically, a company allocates indirect expenses in the same proportion as the direct salary costs for that department or function. Thus, when a number of cost centers are involved in one function, indirect costs are allocated based on each cost center's share of the total payroll. For example, assume that an insurer has four cost centers—A, B, C, and D—and that each center has a specified percentage of employee salaries for a particular function:

Cost center	Percent of salaries
A	60
B	20
C	15
D	5
Total	100

If the insurer is unable to track direct usage of office supplies by each cost center, then the insurer can allocate office supply expenses in the same proportion as the salary expense. Therefore, 60 percent of office supply expenses would be allocated to Cost Center A, 20 percent to Cost Center B, 15 percent to Cost Center C, and 5 percent to Cost Center D.

A department that engages in an insurance company's revenue-generating activities is often called a ***production department*** or an *operating department*. The marketing, underwriting, policy issue, premium collection, policyowner service, and claims administration departments are typical operating departments in an insurance company in that all costs incurred by an operating department are directly traceable to that department. On the other hand, a ***service department*** provides support services to production departments and to other service departments but does not itself generate revenue. Examples of service departments include accounting, actuarial, human resources, legal, and information services. A service department's costs are indirect costs, which should be allocated to the cost centers that use the services. Companies typically use one of several methods of allocating service department costs, as shown in Figure 6-8. Keep in mind that these allocation methods do not add costs to service departments. Rather, these methods are used to redistribute costs to the appropriate service department.

FIGURE 6-8. Allocation Methods: Service Department Costs.

DIRECT METHOD	The ***direct method*** of cost allocation assumes that a service department benefits production departments only. There is no consideration given to services provided by one service department to another.
STEP METHOD	The ***step method*** of cost allocation, also called *step-down allocation*, assumes that service departments perform services for production departments and for other service departments. For instance, the human resources department performs personnel functions for the accounting department, as well as for the underwriting and premium collection departments. Under the step method, a service department's costs are allocated to other benefiting service departments first, and then to benefiting production departments.
RECIPROCAL METHOD	The ***reciprocal method***, also called the *simultaneous method*, of cost allocation, fully recognizes the services that service departments perform for each other. The reciprocal method is thus regarded as more accurate than either the direct method or the step method. Unlike the other methods, the reciprocal method requires the allocation of costs back and forth between all service departments.
CHARGEBACK	Using ***chargeback***, a department allocates its indirect costs to departments based on usage. Chargebacks can be thought of as internal billing. When one department performs work for another department, the first department bills the second department. Chargebacks are most common for corporate service functions such as information processing, building services, accounting, human resources, and office services.

Key Terms and Concepts

cost accounting
differential cost
sunk cost
committed cost
discretionary cost
fixed cost
variable cost
semi-variable cost
unit cost
standard cost
favorable variance
unfavorable variance
marginal cost
marginal unit cost
out-of-pocket cost
opportunity cost
cost accumulation
line of business
function
functional costs
allocation base
time analysis
production department
service department
direct method
step method
reciprocal method
chargeback

Chapter 7

Cost Analysis

Chapter Outline

Comparative Analysis
- Horizontal Analysis
- Trend Analysis
- Vertical Analysis
- Benchmarking

Activity-Based Costing
- Functional Cost Analysis
- Functional Cost Accounting System Development
- Functional Unit Costs

Product Costs and Product Prices

Cost-Volume-Profit Analysis
- Contribution Margin
- Breakeven Point
- Uses of Cost-Volume-Profit Information
- Segment Margin
- Segment Margin Ratio
- Contribution Margin Ratio

Objectives

After reading this chapter, you should be able to

- Differentiate between horizontal analysis and vertical analysis
- Use an index number and trend analysis to analyze trends
- Compare common methods of cost analysis
- Recognize a product's breakeven point

As we noted in Chapter 6, insurers use several methods to account for their costs. Companies also analyze the way costs change over time to recognize trends in costs. Analyzing costs helps a company to predict future costs. Chapter 7 discusses several common methods of cost analysis that insurers use for internal management purposes.

Comparative Analysis

A company's financial statements from a specified accounting period do not tell a complete story. However, by comparing two sets of numbers that reflect company operations during the same accounting period or by analyzing the change in an item over time, you can gain insight into the company's financial condition and performance. ***Comparative financial statements*** present data for two or more accounting periods. Comparative financial statements can present the year-to-year changes in terms of absolute numerical amounts and percentages or ratios.

Two common types of comparative analysis are horizontal analysis and vertical analysis.

Horizontal Analysis

Horizontal analysis is a type of financial statement analysis that involves calculating the absolute amount and the percentage of the increase or decrease in a specified financial statement from one reporting period to another. The earliest financial reporting period used in horizontal analysis is known as the ***base period***. To calculate the absolute amount of the change, subtract the base period amount from that of the period under study, then divide the difference by the base period amount, as follows:

$$\textbf{Absolute amount} = \frac{\textbf{(Period under study amount − Base period amount)}}{\textbf{(Base period amount)}}$$

To calculate the percentage change, we multiply the absolute amount by 100, as follows:

$$\textbf{Percentage change} = \frac{\textbf{(Period under study amount − Base period amount)}}{\textbf{(Base period amount)}} \times 100$$

Figure 7-1 presents an example of how to use horizontal analysis of total assets on a company's balance sheet. Note that similar calculations can be made for every item in the company's financial statements.

Trend Analysis

A ***trend*** is a change that occurs over time. ***Trend analysis***, also called *trend percentages* or *index-number trend analysis,* is a specific type of horizontal analysis that involves calculating percentage changes in financial statement items over several successive accounting periods, rather than over just two periods. Comparative financial statements indicate the direction and velocity of trends. *Direction* refers to whether a trend displays an increase or decrease in an account. *Velocity* refers to whether the increase or decrease in an account is gradual or rapid.

To conduct trend analysis, use the following procedure:

1. Select a base period and assign it an index number of 100 percent. An ***index number*** is a number that provides a statistical method for measuring the change in a variable.

2. Calculate a series of index numbers for the other periods in relation to the base period.

Use the following rules to interpret index numbers:

- An index number greater than 100 indicates an increase in a variable from the base period. For example, an index number of 120 indicates a 20 percent increase from the base period.

FIGURE 7-1. Horizontal Analysis of the Balance Sheet.

BALANCE SHEET

			Increase (Decrease)	
Total Assets	2001	2000	Amount	Percentage
	$14,825,060	$13,901,278	$923,782	6.6

In this example, the insurer had total assets of $13,901,278 in 2000 and total assets of $14,825,060 in 2001. The year 2000 is the base period and the year 2001 is the period under study. The insurer experienced a 6.6 percent increase in total assets from 2000 to 2001, as follows:

$$\frac{(\$14,825,060 - \$13,901,278)}{\$13,901,278} = 0.066 \times 100 = 6.6\%$$

- An index number less than 100 indicates a decrease in the variable from the base period. For example, an index number of 80 indicates a 20 percent decrease from the base period.

Figure 7-2 presents an insurance example of trend analysis.

Vertical Analysis

Vertical analysis is a type of financial statement analysis that reveals the relationship of each financial statement item to a specified

FIGURE 7-2. Trend Analysis: Premium Income and Benefit Payments.

The following information shows life insurance premium income received and life insurance benefits paid during the past five years:

($000s)

	1997	1998	1999	2000	2001
Premium income	2,300	3,700	3,500	4,400	6,000
Benefit payments	1,467	2,295	2,201	3,018	4,020

During the five-year period, premium income and benefits paid increased every year except 1999. We use trend analysis to determine how rapidly premium income increased or decreased and how those trends compare with the increases or decreases in benefits paid. The base period is 1997.

To determine the index numbers for premium income, divide the current year balance by the base year balance of $2,300, then multiply this result by 100. To determine the index numbers for benefit payments, divide the current year balance by the base period figure of $1,467, then multiply this result by 100. The index numbers for premium income and benefit payments for the five-year period are

	1997	1998	1999	2000	2001
Premium income	100%	161%	152%	191%	261%
Benefit payments	100%	156%	150%	206%	274%

In 1998 and 1999, premium income outpaced benefit payments relative to the base period. This trend reversed in 2000 and 2001. Note also that the percentage change in premium income between the base year and 2000 is 52 percent (index 152 – index 100 = 52). However, the percentage change between 1999 and 2000 is *not* 39 percent, as you might assume from a direct comparison (index 191 – index 152). The percentage change between these two years is found by computing the change with reference to 1999 as the "new" base period. The correct percentage change between 2000 and 2001 is 26 percent ($4,400 ÷ $3,500 = index 126), not 39 percent.

financial statement item during the same reporting period. The following table summarizes how to conduct vertical analysis of the balance sheet and the income statement.

Balance Sheet	Income Statement
Divide asset item by total assets	Divide revenue item by total revenues
Divide liabilities and owners' equity item by total liabilities and owners' equity	Divide expense item by total revenues

Let's look at an example of vertical analysis. Figure 7-3 presents an example of how to conduct vertical analysis of the balance sheet to determine the relationship of an insurer's debt securities to its total assets.

We can also use vertical analysis to compile a ***common-size financial statement***, which is a financial statement that consists of the percentages obtained from vertical analysis. Common-size financial statements display only percentages; monetary amounts for each item are not given. The balance sheet and the income statement are often exhibited as common-size statements. Each line item on a common-size balance sheet is expressed as a percentage of (1) total assets or (2) total liabilities plus owners' equity. In other words, total assets is the "common size" to which we relate the balance sheet's other asset amounts. Total liabilities and owners' equity is the "common size" to which we relate the balance sheet's liabilities and owners' equity.

Because amounts on common-size financial statements are stated in relative terms rather than in absolute terms, the use of common-size statements facilitates comparison of companies of different sizes in the same industry. It also facilitates somewhat the comparison of companies in different industries. Suppose Company A's net income is three times that of Company B. You might assume that Company A is the more profitable company. However, by examining common-size income statements for both companies, you might discover that Company B's net income represents a greater percentage of its total revenues than that of Company A. Thus, although Company B's net income is lower, we can deduce from this one comparison that Company B appears to be operating more efficiently than Company A.

Benchmarking

Common-size financial statements are useful for benchmarking purposes. ***Benchmarking*** is an analytical process wherein an insurer selects a number of other companies to use as a "best-practices" standard for comparison with the insurer's own operations and expenses. To

FIGURE 7-3. Vertical Analysis of the Balance Sheet.

In this example, debt securities have a balance of $12,204,000 in 2001. Total assets for 2001 equal $14,825,060. Thus, the insurer's debt securities represent 82.3 percent ($12,204,000 ÷ $14,825,060) of total assets in 2001.

	2001		2000	
	Amount	Percent	Amount	Percent
Assets				
Securities available for sale:				
Debt securities	$12,204,000	82.3%	$11,225,000	80.7%
Equity securites	500,380	3.4%	1,066,800	7.7%
Total Securities Available for Sale	$12,704,380	85.7%	$12,291,800	88.4%
Policy loans	1,392,580	9.4%	824,995	5.9%
Cash and cash equivalents	634,696	4.3%	718,200	5.2%
Property and equipment	93,404	0.6%	66,283	0.5%
Total Assets	$14,825,060	100%	$13,901,278	100%
Liabilities and Stockholders' Equity				
Liabilities:				
Policy liabilities:				
Future policy benefits:				
Life	$ 7,018,245	47.3%	$ 6,983,486	50.2%
Health	3,315,422	22.4%	3,055,782	22.0%
Unpaid claims	122,894	0.8%	104,800	0.8%
Total Policy Liabilities	$ 10,456,561	70.5%	$10,144,068	73.0%
Accounts payable	193,732	1.3%	94,380	0.7%
Due to reinsurers	124,730	0.9%	120,019	0.9%
Dividends payable to stockholders	272,511	1.9%	243,100	1.7%
Long-term liabilities	123,558	0.8%	89,543	0.6%
Total Liabilities	$11,171,092	75.4%	$10,691,110	76.9%
Stockholders' Equity:				
Common stock, par	$ 20,000	0.1%	$ 20,000	0.1%
Additional paid-in capital	641,356	4.3%	641,356	4.7%
Unrealized capital gain (loss), net	112,230	0.8%	100,950	0.7%
Retained earnings	2,880,382	19.4%	2,447,862	17.6%
Total Stockholders' Equity	$ 3,653,968	24.6%	$ 3,210,168	23.1%
Total Liabilities and Stockholder's Equity	$14,825,060	100%	$13,901,278	100%

conduct expense analysis using benchmarking, an insurer determines a set of selection criteria, selects a group of appropriate companies for its comparison studies, and then acquires data regarding their experience with expense distribution by product, line of business, function, or other classification. Insurers commonly benchmark against other insurance companies, against other financial services organizations—such as banks and mutual fund companies—and even against companies in other industries.

Activity-Based Costing

Activity-based costing (ABC) involves linking costs to products based on the activities consumed in producing the products or services. In other words, ABC first traces activities to their costs, then traces the resulting costs to products or lines of business. Activity-based costing uses special terminology, which is presented in Figure 7-4.

Activity-based costing identifies the cost of each activity within a particular function, then assigns the activity costs to the appropriate products. ABC differs from traditional accounting systems, which assume that *products* generate costs. ABC assumes that *activities* generate costs. To provide products, a company engages in activities. These activities consume resources—labor, supplies, computer time,

FIGURE 7-4. Activity-Based Costing Terminology.

An ***activity*** is any procedure that generates work. Activities within a life insurance company include processing a policy application, sending a premium due notice, and investigating a claim.

An ***activity cost*** is the cost attributable to a specified activity. Telephone charges are an activity cost of an insurer's customer service call center.

A ***value-added activity*** is one that makes the product more valuable to the customer. Costs associated with value-added activities typically can be passed through to a company's customers in the form of higher prices.

A ***non-value-added activity*** is one that does not make the product or service more valuable to the customer. Non-value-added activities are wasteful and should be minimized because a company cannot pass along the cost of such activities to its customers.

An ***activity driver*** is the output of an activity being performed. It is the purpose that propels the activity. For example, if the activity is policy application processing, the activity driver would be a processed policy application.

and so on—and produce outputs, such as a check for an approved claim. ABC identifies each activity, calculates the costs of performing each unit of activity, and then assigns the cost of each unit of activity to a unit of output or production.

The primary benefits of ABC are that it provides a solid basis for assigning costs to products and assists management in identifying non-value-added activities. ABC enables company management to report the cost of performing specific tasks or activities. Thus, through ABC, management can assign these costs to specified products more effectively than under traditional costing systems. The intended result of ABC is more appropriate pricing and more effective cost control.

Generally, establishing an ABC system involves several steps, as shown in Figure 7-5. Figure 7-6 shows a simple comparison of costs accumulated in a traditional way and costs accumulated by activity. Note that the bottom line is the same. In other words, total costs incurred do not change.

FIGURE 7-5. Activity-Based Costing: Steps and Examples.

	STEPS	EXAMPLE
1	*Identify activities.*	Activities for claims verification typically include separate tasks, such as making telephone calls, photocopying, and preparing affidavits. Activities in turn are assigned to activity centers, which are similar to cost centers in a traditional cost accounting system.
2	*Identify the activity drivers for each activity.*	Activity drivers in insurance companies include policies issued, premiums processed, and policies changed.
3	*Match each cost to each activity by finding a unit cost for each activity driver.*	Suppose the activity driver is applications submitted, and the activity caused by the driver is the underwriting process. In this case, the insurer's managers first total the actual costs involved in the underwriting process by tracking the time involved in underwriting, as well as accumulating all relevant costs for employee salaries, equipment, and supplies.
4	*Determine the unit cost of each activity for comparative purposes.*	The insurer wants to determine the unit cost of underwriting one policy. To calculate the per policy cost, divide total underwriting costs by the number of applications underwritten. Suppose 350 applications are submitted during the accounting period and the insurer's total underwriting costs are $43,750 for the period. The unit cost for underwriting one application is $125: $43,750 total underwriting costs ÷ 350 policy applications submitted.
5	*Assign each activity cost to the smallest organizational unit for which it has meaning.*	The activity costs for underwriting group life insurance policies would be assigned to the group life insurance line of business.

FIGURE 7-6. Comparison of Traditional Costing and Activity-Based Costing.

Traditional Costs (by Category)

Salaries	$500,000
Supplies	70,000
Rent	60,000
Information Systems	55,000
Miscellaneous	25,000
	$710,000

Activity-Based Costs

Underwrite applications	$185,000
Process approved applications	90,000
Process claims	95,000
Issue claim checks	75,000
Service policyowner requests	130,000
Manage departments	80,000
File statements with regulators	55,000
	$710,000

Functional Cost Analysis

As we discussed in Chapter 6, functional costs are the total activity costs within a function, regardless of which department or cost center incurred the costs. A company's cost accounting system should be designed to support functional cost analysis. ***Functional cost analysis***, a subset of activity-based costing, involves the process of accumulating the costs that are involved in each activity within a function. For example, functional cost analysis requires an insurer to gather the following types of costs associated with the function of collecting renewal premiums:

- Cost data from the automated processes associated with receiving and recording premium income
- Machine costs for preparing and mailing premium notices
- Selling costs and administrative costs by product line
- Other indirect costs incurred by any department involved in collecting renewal premiums

An insurer's accounting system should accumulate costs for workflow processes, organizational structures, or departments. Insurers use functional cost analysis to

- Price products
- Monitor and control current operational procedures
- Identify trends that are not recognizable with conventional forms of analysis

- Develop more accurate budget estimates
- Benchmark operations against other companies

Functional Cost Accounting System Development

Developing a functional cost accounting system requires a specified level of detail. The system must be able to identify each function within the company—marketing, claims processing, information processing, underwriting, etc.—as well as each line of business or product offered. These functions, lines of business, or products may or may not coincide with the departmental units of the company. For example, mail handling is typically a function of one department in the company's organizational structure. On the other hand, the policy issue function could be administered by a single subdivision of one department or it could span two or more departments.

When developing a functional cost accounting system, system designers must be careful to include all activities and costs—and only those activities and costs—that are relevant to the specific function under study. The entire functional cost accounting system should be flexible enough to change along with company growth or diversification. The system should also be able to provide for exceptions and peculiarities within any function or line of business.

Functional Unit Costs

One of the most useful ways to analyze functional costs is through the use of functional unit costs. Recall from Chapter 6 that a unit cost is the incurred expense attributable to a single measured amount of work. A ***functional unit cost*** is a type of functional cost that is calculated by dividing the total functional cost by an appropriate base unit. The appropriate unit of measure to use in calculating functional unit costs depends on both the function and the line of business being analyzed. Units of measure may be monetary or non-monetary in nature. Figure 7-7 shows some typical insurance company functions and the units of measure that may be used to express the functional unit cost.

Product Costs and Product Prices

Cost is a major factor in designing a company's products. A specific insurance product's income from premiums and investments may

FIGURE 7-7. Insurer Functions and Functional Unit Costs.

Policy issue costs can be expressed in terms of the number of policies issued, the number of applications submitted, or the face amount of insurance (per $1,000) issued.

Function	Unit of Measure
Sales	First-year premiums New policies issued
Selection and issue	Policies issued New business (face amount)
Policy maintenance	Policies in force Renewal premiums
Research and development	Premiums Policies in force (face amount)
Underwriting	Per application Per policy issued
Agent's compensation	First-year premiums Renewal premiums

have to cover many types of costs. Understanding cost behavior is essential to estimating a product's costs. Some costs typically decrease over time as a company gains product and marketing experience. Other costs can escalate rapidly, particularly in times of high inflation, and quickly reduce or even eliminate the profit expected from a particular product. We discussed the classification of costs by behavior in Chapter 6. One tool that managers use to help analyze the appropriateness of their pricing decisions is cost-volume-profit analysis.

Cost-Volume-Profit Analysis

Three critical elements in making business decisions are cost, volume, and profit. Analysis of these elements is a powerful management accounting tool. ***Cost-volume-profit (CVP) analysis***, sometimes called *breakeven analysis* or *profit-volume analysis*, is the study of the effects of changes in product prices, sales volume, fixed costs, variable costs, and the type of products a company offers. In the context of CVP analysis, ***volume*** is the quantity of sales that is associated with the product being analyzed. CVP analysis assists managers in planning and budgeting. CVP analysis helps answer questions such as

- Which products and services should we sell?
- What costs are associated with each product we offer?
- What price should we charge for each product?
- What level of sales volume can we expect to achieve?

Contribution Margin

CVP analysis makes use of costs that are classified by behavior—fixed costs, variable costs, and semi-variable costs—and unit costs, which we discussed in Chapter 6. Fundamental to CVP analysis is the concept of ***contribution margin***, which is the difference between a product's selling price and its variable costs. To calculate a product's contribution margin, a company must separate the product's fixed costs—such as rent, utilities, and some employee salaries—from its variable costs—such as agent commissions and operating expenses.

The term *contribution* is used because this amount is available to (1) cover fixed costs and (2) contribute to profit. In this context, a ***margin*** is the excess of a product's revenues over its costs. Note that a product can have a net loss, in which the product's costs exceed its revenues. The company can also break even or experience a net gain on the product. Two ways to express contribution margin are total contribution margin and unit contribution margin, as follows:

Total contribution margin = Sales revenue – Total variable costs
Unit contribution margin = Unit price – Unit variable cost

In this discussion, we state the unit price of an insurance product as the price per $1,000 of coverage or the price per policy.

Breakeven Point

The contribution margin indicates the impact of changes in a company's profit that result from changes in costs, selling prices, volume, or a combination of these factors. The point at which a product's revenues are equal to its costs is called the ***breakeven point***. At the breakeven point, total revenues equal total costs, and fixed costs equal the contribution margin. The breakeven point could be found by trial and error. However, a simpler approach is to use a breakeven formula, in which fixed costs are divided by the unit contribution margin:

$$\text{Breakeven point} = \frac{\text{Fixed costs}}{\text{Unit contribution margin}}$$

For clarity, this equation is often rewritten as:

$$\text{Breakeven point} = \frac{\text{Fixed costs}}{\text{Unit price} - \text{Unit variable cost}}$$

Figure 7-8 provides an example of the calculation of a product's breakeven point.

Insight 7-1 describes the application of a cost-volume-profit graph in determining a product's breakeven point.

Uses of Cost-Volume-Profit Information

CVP analysis has many applications for management accounting, because it enables a company's managers to test scenarios using different cost, volume, and price assumptions for each product so they can maximize the net gain to the company. CVP analysis seeks the most profitable combination of fixed cost, variable cost, sales volume, and product price. Managers study changes in any or all of these variables to maximize the performance of their products, product lines, and organizations.

Contribution margin is an important consideration in CVP analysis because an increase in a company's net gain from operations must come from an increase in contribution margin. Ways to increase contribution margin include (1) decreasing a product's selling price to a point where an increase in sales volume increases total revenues, (2) increasing the product's fixed costs to support an increase in sales volume, or (3) balancing fixed costs and variable costs to achieve appropriate changes in sales volume. The process is more complex when companies sell many products. In that case, improving a company's net gain from operations comes from finding the right volume of each product to sell.

Segment Margin

Besides calculating and analyzing the contribution margin on each product, a company may calculate the segment margin for various segments of each profit center. A ***segment margin*** is the portion of

FIGURE 7-8. Breakeven Point.

Suppose the Value Life Insurance Company sells a whole life insurance product that has a unit premium (sales price) of $1 per $1,000 of face amount of insurance and a unit variable cost of $0.60 per $1,000 of face amount per month. The unit contribution margin for this product is $0.40 ($1.00 – $0.60). If Value sells 2,000,000 whole life policies during a specified accounting period and has $400,000 in fixed costs per month, the net gain on this product for the accounting period is $400,000, as shown on the following contribution income statement:

	Per unit	Total
Sales revenue (2,000,000 policies)	$1.00	$ 2,000,000
Less: Variable costs	$0.60	(1,200,000)
Contribution margin	$0.40	$ 800,000
Less: Fixed costs		(400,000)
Net gain (loss)		$ 400,000

When Value sells just enough units of the product to recover its investment in the product, it will break even on the product. The breakeven point is at 1,000,000 units sold, as follows:

	Total
Sales revenue (1,000,000 units)	$ 1,000,000
Less: Variable costs	(600,000)
Contribution margin	$ 400,000
Less: Fixed costs	(400,000)
Net gain (loss)	$ 0

After Value reaches the breakeven sales level of 1,000,000 policies sold, Value will begin to experience a net gain equal to the contribution margin for each additional policy sold. Thus, if Value sells 1,000,001 units, or one more policy than its breakeven point, its net gain is 40 cents, as follows:

	Total
Sales revenue (1,000,001 units)	$1,000,001.00
Less: Variable costs	(600,000.60)
Contribution margin	$ 400,000.40
Less: Fixed costs	(400,000.00)
Net gain (loss)	$ 0.40

Substituting the appropriate values into this equation verifies that Value's breakeven point for the whole life insurance product is 1,000,000 units, as follows:

$$\textbf{Breakeven point} = \frac{\$400{,}000}{(\$1.00 - \$0.60)} = \textbf{1,000,000 policies}$$

the contribution margin that remains after a segment has covered its direct fixed costs. In this context, a ***segment*** is a product, line of business, or responsibility center. The segment margin is calculated

Insight 7-1. The Cost-Volume-Profit Graph.

Companies often prepare CVP data graphically. The ***cost-volume-profit (CVP) graph***, sometimes called a *breakeven chart*, highlights CVP relationships over a wide range of sales levels. The CVP graph gives managers another way to see the point at which a product's net gain begins. A CVP graph plots unit volume along the horizontal (x) axis, and unit price along the vertical (y) axis. Preparing the CVP graph is a three-step process:

- Plot fixed costs as a straight horizontal line at the appropriate level for the period.
- Draw a total cost line (fixed costs + variable costs) by applying the variable unit cost to the number of units produced. Note that, at zero sales volume, total costs equal fixed costs.
- Draw a sales revenue line, again by applying the number of units sold to the selling price.

Only a few points must be plotted on the CVP graph before you are able to determine the correct steepness of each line. The point at which the total cost line and the sales revenue line intersect is the breakeven point. If a company achieves a level of sales to the left of (or less than) the breakeven point, the company experiences a net loss on the product. If sales reach a level to the right of (or greater than) the breakeven point, then the company experiences a net gain.

Let's look at the CVP graph for Value's whole life insurance product. Note that the total cost line and the sales revenue line intersect when the volume of sales is 1,000,000 policies. This is the same breakeven point that we calculated using the breakeven formula. At each volume of sales to the right of the breakeven point, the vertical distance between the sales revenue line and the total cost line is the amount of net gain realized at that volume. Likewise, to the left of the breakeven point, the vertical distance between the total cost line and the sales revenue line is the amount of net loss realized at that volume.

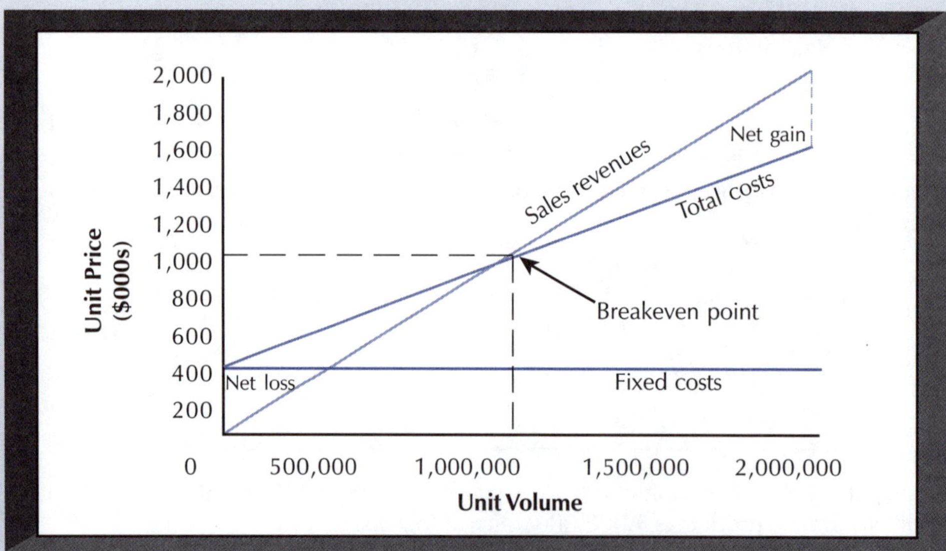

by subtracting the segment's direct fixed costs from its contribution margin, as follows:

Segment margin = Contribution margin – Direct fixed costs

A segment margin indicates the segment's profitability. If a segment cannot recover its own costs, then it cannot be profitable.

Therefore, a segment margin should be positive—that is, greater than zero. Typically, a segment produces a segment report, in which total costs—both fixed costs and variable costs—incurred by the segment are subtracted from the segment's total revenues. The segment report divides fixed costs into direct costs and indirect costs to allow for the calculation of a segment margin. Figure 7-9 depicts segment reports and the segment margin.

FIGURE 7-9. Segment Reports and the Segment Margin.

The Turnstone Life Insurance Company is organized into profit centers that are segmented by product line into group life insurance and ordinary life insurance. The ordinary life product line is in turn segmented into two product forms: (1) term life insurance and (2) whole life insurance. The whole life product form is segmented into two products: (2a) traditional whole life insurance and (2b) universal life insurance. Note that all of Turnstone's segments are profitable because they all have positive segment margins. For simplicity, we show only actual amounts. In practice, Turnstone's segment reports would show both budgeted amounts and actual amounts, as well as the variances between them.

Product Line Segments of Turnstone Life Insurance Company	**Total Company**	**Group Life**	**Ordinary Life**
Total revenues	$6,949,176	$4,308,489	$2,640,687
Less: Variable costs:			
Variable policy benefits	3,207,111	2,151,479	1,055,632
Other variable costs	244,476	171,133	73,343
Total Variable Costs	$3,451,587	$2,322,612	$1,128,975
Contribution margin	$3,497,589	$1,985,877	$1,511,712
Less: Direct fixed costs	622,811	404,827	217,984
Product line segment margin	$2,874,778	$1,581,050	$1,293,728
Less: Indirect fixed costs	1,692,314		
Income Before Taxes	$1,182,464		

Product Form Segments of Ordinary Life Product Line	**Ordinary Life**	**Term Life**	**Whole Life**
Total revenues	$2,640,687	$ 422,510	$2,218,177
Less: Variable costs:			
Variable policy benefits	1,055,632	190,014	865,618
Other variable costs	73,343	24,203	49,140
Total Variable Costs	$1,128,975	$ 214,217	$ 914,758
Contribution margin	$1,511,712	$ 208,293	$1,303,419
Less: Direct fixed costs	161,445	32,289	129,156
Product line segment margin	$1,350,267	$ 176,004	$1,174,263
Less: Indirect fixed costs	56,539		
Income Before Taxes	$1,293,728		

Figure 7-9. Segment Reports and the Segment Margin (continued).

Product Item Segments of Whole Life Product Form	**Whole Life**	**Traditional Whole Life**	**Universal Life**
Total revenues	$2,218,177	$1,774,542	$ 443,635
Less: Variable costs:			
Variable policy benefits	865,618	675,182	190,436
Other variable costs	49,140	34,398	14,742
Total Variable Costs	$ 914,758	$ 709,580	$ 205,178
Contribution margin	$1,303,419	$1,064,962	$ 238,457
Less: Direct fixed costs	87,872	73,813	14,059
Product line segment margin	$1,215,547	$ 991,149	$ 224,395
Less: Indirect fixed costs	41,284		
Product Form Segment Margin	$1,174,263		

These segment reports are similar to other responsibility reports in that the direct costs attributable to one responsibility manager are greater than the sum of the direct costs of the responsibility centers under that manager's supervision. For example, the direct costs attributable to the responsibility manager of Turnstone's ordinary life insurance product line segment are greater than the direct fixed costs attributed to the ordinary life product form segment, as shown in the following table:

Product form segment	Direct fixed costs	$161,445
Product form segment	Indirect fixed costs	$ 56,539
Product line segment	Direct fixed costs	$217,984

Segment Margin Ratio

Segment margins, when put in ratio form, are also useful for performance evaluation purposes. The ***segment margin ratio***, a measure of a segment's efficiency of operating performance, is calculated by dividing the segment margin by the segment's total revenues, as follows:

Segment margin ratio = Segment margin ÷ Segment's total revenues

Contribution Margin Ratio

The ***contribution margin ratio***, a measure of segment performance, is calculated by dividing the contribution margin by the segment's total revenues, as follows:

Contribution margin ratio = Contribution margin ÷ Segment's total revenues

Calculating both the segment margin ratio and the contribution margin ratio enables a company's managers to compare segments of different sizes. Figure 7-10 depicts the segment margin ratios and contribution margin ratios for Turnstone's term life and whole life product forms.

FIGURE 7-10. Segment Margin Ratio and Contribution Margin Ratio.

	Segment Margin Ratio		Contribution Margin Ratio	
	Ratio	Percentage	Ratio	Percentage
Term Life	$ 176,004 $ 422,510	41.7	$ 208,293 $ 422,510	49.3
Whole Life	$1,174,263 $2,218,177	52.9	$1,303,419 $2,218,177	58.8

Key Terms and Concepts

comparative financial statements
horizontal analysis
base period
trend
trend analysis
index number
vertical analysis
common-size financial statement
benchmarking
activity-based costing (ABC)
activity
activity cost
value-added activity
non-value-added activity
activity driver
functional cost analysis
functional unit cost
cost-volume-profit (CVP) analysis
volume
contribution margin
margin
breakeven point
cost-volume-profit (CVP) graph
segment margin
segment
segment margin ratio
contribution margin ratio

Chapter 8

Budgeting

Chapter Outline

Why Budget?

Budgeting Approaches
- Top-Down Budgeting and Bottom-Up Budgeting
- Zero-Based Budgeting

Budget Classifications
- Static Budgets and Flexible Budgets
- Short-Term Budgets and Long-Term Budgets
- Rolling Budgets and Period Budgets

Types of Budgets
- Operational Budgets
- Cash Budgets
- Capital Budgets
- Pro Forma Financial Statements

OBJECTIVES

After reading this chapter, you should be able to

- Describe the benefits and disadvantages of budgeting
- Identify the relative strengths of top-down budgeting, bottom-up budgeting, and zero-based budgeting
- Distinguish between static budgets and flexible budgets, short-term budgets and long-term budgets, and rolling budgets and period budgets
- Recognize the main components of a master budget
- Describe the purpose of capital budgeting
- Explain the purpose of pro forma financial statements

Through budgeting, a company affirms its goals and establishes expected performance levels for its management team. ***Budgeting*** is a management accounting process that includes creating a financial plan of action that an organization believes will help achieve its goals. A ***budget*** is a financial plan of action, expressed in monetary terms, which covers a specified time period, such as one year. After a budget is created, a company uses the budget to monitor performance. Budgets contain estimates that reflect management's expectations of a company's future performance. Budgets provide a company with a point of reference. A company can compare actual results to budgeted expectations, and the company can gain insights that help plan new or improved courses of action.

Why Budget?

All companies budget, however informally. Budgets outline a company's plans for its financial resources. Budgets also indicate whether company managers are achieving the company's strategic and operational goals. A primary objective of a budget is to systematically project—for a given department, division, or line of business—the anticipated revenues and expenses during a specified accounting period. The budgeting process enables a company to

- Monitor and evaluate ongoing operations
- Evaluate managerial performance
- Assist in financial planning
- Control and reduce expenses
- Communicate information throughout the company
- Motivate employees

Although budgeting has many benefits, budgeting also has some disadvantages, including the potential for management to

- Consume time that might otherwise be spent more "productively"
- Spend the entire budgeted amount, even when unnecessary
- Establish unrealistic budget expectations
- Become discouraged from experimenting with innovative solutions to changing market conditions

Job descriptions and management salaries are often based on how much money managers have in their budget. To maintain or improve their status in a company, managers may pad their budgets. Typically, padding occurs when responsibility managers budget for higher expenses than they expect to incur during the accounting period. Sometimes managers use the budgeting process to improve or protect their status in a company, without regard to the effect that such actions may have on the company's goals. A responsibility manager may pad a budget by understating expected revenues or overstating expected expenses. In this case, the manager makes achieving revenue goals easier.

Budget manipulation can also affect a responsibility center's expenses. Excessive year-end spending typically occurs when a responsibility manager acts to avoid losing budgeted expense levels for the next accounting period. In this case, managers believe they must spend all money budgeted for expenses by a specified date to receive at least the same amount or level of budgeted expenses in the next accounting period.

The budgeting process requires much planning to be successful. In many companies, a budget committee formed by top executives and managers from the company's main functions oversees the budgeting process. The budget committee reviews proposed budgets for reasonableness and works toward integrating all responsibility center budgets into the master budget. Ultimately, the budget committee provides the overall guidance necessary to coordinate a company-wide budgeting process.

Budgeting Approaches

Companies typically undertake one or more of three approaches to the budgeting process: (1) top-down budgeting, (2) bottom-up budgeting, and (3) zero-based budgeting. In practice, most companies use a combination of these approaches in a manner that best suits the company's culture and needs.

Top-Down Budgeting and Bottom-Up Budgeting

Top-down budgeting begins with a company's senior management and is passed down to lower-level management. The monetary amounts found in top-down budgets are based on senior management's strategic plan, as well as financial information about the company's activities in prior years. ***Bottom-up budgeting*** is generated in each department or responsibility center by lower-level managers and is presented in the form of recommendations to senior management.

Bottom-up budgeting typically includes a larger number of company employees—and takes considerably more time—than does top-down budgeting.

Top-down budgeting is more likely than bottom-up budgeting to reflect top management's intentions for the company. On the other hand, bottom-up budgets reflect the input and participation of the employees who will be responsible for achieving the company's goals. Thus, bottom-up budgeting is more likely to reflect the realities of the company's core business operations. Moreover, bottom-up budgeting often has more grassroots support among company employees than does top-down budgeting. Despite the differences between top-down budgeting and bottom-up budgeting, the previous year's budget is typically a starting point for making adjustments to the next year's budget, regardless of which of these two approaches is used.

Zero-Based Budgeting

Companies can apply top-down and bottom-up budgeting approaches to both revenue and expense budgets. Zero-based budgeting generally applies only to a company's expense budgets. Under ***zero-based budgeting (ZBB),*** a company begins with the premise that no resources will be allocated for the next accounting period unless and until each expense is shown to be in accord with the company's strategic and operational goals. For every accounting period, each responsibility center or line of business must justify its continued existence and operation.

In essence, ZBB treats each activity and function as though it is a new project under consideration. Unlike the top-down and bottom-up budgeting approaches, ZBB does not automatically assume that current-year expense levels are reasonable starting points for developing the expense budget for the next accounting period. Instead, cost analysis is imposed on all levels of management to evaluate each activity in terms of efficiency and need. Lower-level employees play a key role in ZBB because they are often called upon to provide details that help a company to assess the importance and financial requirements of each activity. Other benefits of ZBB include the breadth and quality of financial information contained in budgets and the training and education employees receive as part of their contribution to the ZBB process.

The main disadvantage of using ZBB is that it is both costly and time consuming. Much work associated with ZBB involves (1) collecting and analyzing data to justify each item and (2) preparing contingency budgets in case unanticipated expenses arise. For this reason, many companies use a modified ZBB process. With a modified ZBB approach, for example, ZBB is applied to specified activities or functions, or is performed every other year.

Budget Classifications

Regardless of the budgeting approach a company uses, each budget can be classified as (1) a static budget or a flexible budget, (2) a short-term budget or a long-term budget, and (3) a rolling budget or a period budget.

Static Budgets and Flexible Budgets

When budgets are classified by the degree of variability inherent in them, they are often referred to as either static budgets or flexible budgets. The amounts in a ***static budget***, also known as a *fixed budget* or a *fixed-amount budget*, are generally not subject to change unless management has approved the changes. As a result, static budgets are of limited managerial usefulness if budgeted amounts of revenues and expenses are uncertain. Static budgets provide no alternative financial predictions when actual experience differs from the assumptions underlying the budgeted figures. Static budgets are most useful when a budget's objective is to reduce or limit expenses. Suppose a company allocates $10,000,000 for expenses for the coming month. In this example, the company would not allocate more than $10,000,000 for expenses. The company could, however, spend less than $10,000,000 for expenses.

Figure 8-1 presents an example of a monthly static expense budget for each function of an insurance company.

FIGURE 8-1. A Static Budget.

Expenses by Functional Area ($000s)	
Functional Area	**Budgeted Amount**
Marketing	$ 1,833
Investments	973
Actuarial	237
Underwriting	1,613
Claims administration	442
Accounting	247
Legal	377
Policyowner service	772
Human resources	1,746
Information systems	1,760
Total Expenses	$10,000

In contrast, a ***flexible budget***, also known as a *flexible-amount budget*, a *dynamic budget*, or a *variable budget*, provides alternative sets of budget estimates to use under different circumstances that may arise during an accounting period. Managers generally use flexible budgets to test assumptions. When an insurer cannot predict accurately its income and expenses for a given period—such as during the introduction of a new product or line of business—the insurer might prepare separate budgets for levels of activity that approximate different projected dollar amounts of insurance sold.

Suppose an insurer is budgeting first-year commission expenses for a new product. In this case, the insurer cannot forecast with certainty the exact amount of new product sales, so the insurer prepares multiple budgets using different sales projections. Figure 8-2 shows an example of a flexible budget.

Short-Term Budgets and Long-Term Budgets

Budgets can cover almost any time frame. A ***short-term budget,*** also called an *operating budget*, generally covers a period of one year or less and relates mainly to a company's operations during that period. Often, the budget is further divided into quarterly, monthly, weekly, or sometimes daily budgets. A ***long-term budget***, also called a *strategic budget*, generally covers periods of more than one year. Many insurers produce long-term budgets covering the next 5 to 10 years. Budgets projecting that far into the future allow a company to estimate revenues and expenses that correspond to the company's strategic goals. Long-term budgets have less detail than short-term budgets. The most current year of the long-term budget should be the current period's operating budget. Thus, a long-term budget incorporates a company's short-term budgets.

FIGURE 8-2. A Flexible Budget.

Commission Expense Budget
($000s)

	Range of Sales		
	Pessimistic	**Expected**	**Optimistic**
Budgeted sales revenue	$22,000	$25,000	$28,000
Sales level relative to expected	88%	100%	112%
First-year commission expense	$12,100	$13,750	$15,400

Rolling Budgets and Period Budgets

A ***rolling budget***, also known as a *continuous budget*, allows a company to continually maintain projections for a specified time period into the future. A company that uses a six-month rolling budget would update the budget at the end of each month so that budget projections always apply to the coming six-month period. A ***period budget*** covers a specific time frame, such as one month or one year, and expires at the end of that time frame. The figures in a period budget do not change during the time frame covered by the budget. A rolling budget is in essence a series of period budgets. Because a rolling budget is updated regularly based on the results of the most recent period, it can maintain a higher measure of accuracy than a period budget. However, maintaining a rolling budget generally requires more resources than does a period budget. Figure 8-3 depicts a rolling sales revenue budget.

Types of Budgets

The accounting function combines the individual budgets for each department or responsibility center into the company's ***master budget***, which shows the overall operating and financing plans for

FIGURE 8-3. A Rolling Budget.

Suppose the Bountiful Life Insurance Company creates a rolling budget for the period January 1 to June 30. If Bountiful updates the budget monthly, then it presents a new budget on February 1 to reflect the six-month period from that date until July 31. Bountiful repeats this procedure for March 1 to August 31, April 1 to September 30, and so on. Each new budget reflects Bountiful's revised projections for the coming six-month period.

Sales Revenue ($000s)

	Jan	Feb	Mar	Apr	May	Jun	Jul	Aug	Sep	6-Month Total
Sales revenues	$500	$525	$535	$495	$505	$520	–	–	–	$3,080
After 1st month										
Sales revenues	–	$530	$540	$500	$510	$530	$535	–	–	$3,145
After 2nd month										
Sales revenues	–	–	$536	$500	$505	$525	$530	$510	–	$3,106
After 3rd month										
Sales revenues	–	–	–	$512	$515	$535	$540	$520	$540	$3,162

the company during a specified accounting period. Companies refer to the master budget by different names, such as *comprehensive budget*, *corporate budget*, *performance plan*, or simply the *budget*. (A company's master budget can also be thought of as a *profit plan*, because achieving the company's goals should result in a profit for the company.) In this text, we use the term *master budget*. Developing the master budget begins with a forecast of a company's revenues, expenses, cash flows, and capital investment activities. Most companies compile the master budget annually and update it semiannually. The master budget generally consists of several key types of budgets, including (1) operational budgets, (2) cash budgets, and (3) capital budgets, which we discuss in the following sections.

Operational Budgets

Operational budgeting is a budgeting activity that covers all or part of a company's operations. A budget that includes part or all of a company's core business operations is called an ***operational budget***. The operational budget reflects the financial steps the company will take during the coming year to achieve those objectives. Although the format and content of operational budgets vary widely among companies, operational budgets show the revenues or expenses that a company expects during a specified accounting period. Two basic types of operational budgets are revenue budgets and expense budgets.

Revenue Budgets

All operational budgets begin with a forecast of sales revenue and investment income. For life insurance and annuity companies, a ***sales forecast*** is an estimate of insurance and annuity sales for a particular period. An ***investment forecast*** is an estimate of the performance, for a specified period, of bonds, stocks, mortgages, and other invested assets a company own. The company estimates how much money it will earn from both sales and investments so that it has a reasonable idea of how much money will be available. Insurers use one or more forecasting techniques to project sales and investment performance. A detailed discussion of forecasting techniques is beyond the scope of this text.

After developing the sales forecast and the investment forecast, a company then develops its revenue budget. A ***revenue budget*** indicates the amount of income from operations—policy sales and investments—that the company expects in the coming budget period. The revenue budget determines the limits of the other budgets and must be prepared before them. Some insurers divide the revenue budget into the sales budget and the investment budget:

- A ***sales budget*** projects first-year and renewal premium income. The insurer bases its sales budget estimates on historical data, reviews of the marketplace, and premium rates charged by competitors, among other factors. The sales budget is often itemized by product type, such as life insurance and annuities.

- An ***investment budget*** projects the types of investments the insurer will make and the expected amount of investment income for each type of investment. The investment budget is often itemized by investment type, such as bonds, mortgage loans, and stocks.

Figure 8-4 shows a revenue budget, divided into its sales and investment components.

Expense Budgets

After developing its revenue budget, a company then prepares its expense budget. An ***expense budget*** is a schedule of expenses expected during an accounting period. An expense budget is useful in controlling expenses, measuring management performance, and assigning responsibility for expenses. Insight 8-1 describes common types of expense budgets for insurance companies. Figure 8-5 shows an example of an expense budget.

FIGURE 8-4. A Revenue Budget.

Suppose the Quality Life Insurance Company sells individual life insurance, group life insurance, and individual annuities. Quality's annual revenue budget is itemized by quarter. Quarter 1 is shown.

Revenue Budget (\$000s)

	Quarter 1
Premium Income	
Individual insurance	$ 5,008
Individual annuities	4,427
Group insurance	3,606
Total Premium Income	$13,041
Investment Income	
From long-term securities	$ 1,926
From short-term securities	2,735
Mortgage income	1,127
Total Investment Income	$ 5,788
Total Revenues	$18,829

Insight 8-1. Common Expense Budgets.

Benefits budget. A budget that indicates the amount of money the insurer expects to pay for claims, cash surrenders, and policy dividends during the next accounting period. Most expenses in benefits budgets are variable expenses because these expenses depend on sales volume.

Sales expense budget. A budget that indicates the costs incurred in selling insurance. These expenses include commission costs, the costs of advertising, promotion, travel, branch office operations, and salaries for marketing staff. Sales expense budget figures are also typically variable expenses.

General and administrative expense budget. A budget that includes expenses—typically fixed expenses—needed for insurance company operations. Usually, this budget is the sum of all departmental expense budgets. The general and administrative expense budget also includes such company-wide expenses as computer equipment costs and administrative salaries.

Cash Budgets

Budgeting for cash helps a company plan for both cash shortages and cash excesses. ***Cash budgeting*** is a budgeting activity that anticipates the cash flows into and out of a company during an accounting

FIGURE 8-5. An Expense Budget.

Quality's annual expense budget is itemized by quarter. Note that this budget includes elements of the benefits budget, the sales expense budget, and the general and administrative expense budget. Here, only Quarter 1 is shown.

Expense Budget ($000s)

	Quarter 1
Contractual Benefits	
Individual insurance	$ 2,324
Individual annuities	1,755
Group insurance	1,373
Total Contractual Benefits	$5,452
Commissions	$ 2,831
General and Administrative	
Leases	$ 145
Payroll	1,134
General	705
Depreciation	22
Total General and Administrative	$ 2,006
Total Expenses	$10,289

period. Many companies divide the annual cash budget into quarterly, monthly, weekly, and sometimes daily budgets to monitor cash flow more closely. Some insurers generate a daily cash report for the investment function, which uses the report to determine the additional funds available to invest.

A ***cash budget*** is a type of budget that projects a company's beginning cash balance, cash inflows, cash outflows, and ending cash balance for a specified accounting period, typically by quarter. Cash budgets assist company management in deciding the company's investment strategy. Although cash inflows and outflows are unique to each company, we can obtain general assumptions about cash flows for each industry. Insurers also use forecasting techniques to project cash receipts and cash disbursements. A cash budget consists of a cash receipts budget (cash inflows) and a cash disbursement budget (cash outflows).

A company plans for its cash inflows through a ***cash receipts budget***, which is a schedule of cash receipts expected during the accounting period. To predict both the timing and amount of its cash receipts, a company constructs the cash receipts budget using data from both the sales and investments forecasts. Figure 8-6 shows an example of a cash receipts budget.

An insurer estimates the timing and amount of all of its cash disbursements in the ***cash disbursements budget***. Estimating cash disbursements for fixed expenses such as salaries is relatively easy and accurate. Estimating the cash disbursements for variable expenses such as benefit payments and commissions is less predictable. The accuracy of these predictions depends in large part on the accuracy of the sales forecast. Figure 8-7 shows an example of a cash disbursements budget.

After the cash receipts budget and the cash disbursements budget are complete, the next step is to combine them into the cash budget. Information contained in the cash budget includes the

- Beginning cash balance, which equals the ending cash balance from the prior period
- Available cash for the period, which equals the beginning cash balance *plus* cash receipts during the period
- Minimum cash balance, an amount that is determined by the company
- Cash needed for the period, which equals cash disbursements plus the minimum cash balance
- Excess cash or cash shortage, which equals available cash *minus* cash needed for the period
- Amount of any cash borrowed or repaid, including interest

FIGURE 8-6. A Cash Receipts Budget.

The Quality Life Insurance Company divides its cash receipts budget into receipts from sales of insurance and annuity products and receipts from investments. Only Quarter 1 is shown.

Cash Receipts Budget ($000s)	Quarter 1
Policy Receipts	
Individual insurance premiums	$ 5,008
Individual annuity considerations	4,427
Group insurance premiums	3,606
Total Policy Receipts	$13,041
Investment Receipts	
Long-term securities income	$ 1,926
Short-term securities income	2,735
Mortgage income	1,127
Total Investment Receipts	$ 5,788
Total Cash Receipts	$18,829

For simplicity, this cash receipts budget assumes that there is no timing difference between income and cash receipts. In other words, we assume that the cash receipts budget amounts equal those in the revenue budget in Figure 8-4.

- Ending cash balance, which equals excess cash or shortage of cash *plus* any borrowing or repayment activity

The ***minimum cash balance*** is the amount of cash that an insurer determines is necessary to pay all obligations in an accounting period without having excess cash. Setting this figure too low raises the risk of running out of cash. Setting this figure too high carries a high opportunity cost. Recall from Chapter 6 that an opportunity cost is the benefit that is forfeited or given up in choosing one decision alternative over another. Companies that establish a relatively low minimum balance typically invest most of their cash and arrange for a line of credit from a bank to cover any cash shortages. A ***line of credit***, also called a *bank line*, is a prearranged agreement whereby a company can borrow money for a short-term, up to a specified amount. Some insurers keep excess cash in interest-bearing bank accounts, from which the bank automatically transfers money to the insurer's checking account as needed.

FIGURE 8-7. A Cash Disbursements Budget.

Quality divides its cash disbursements budget into disbursements for insurance and annuities, and disbursements for investments. Quality also subdivides the disbursements for insurance and annuities into a fixed component and a variable component.

Cash Disbursements Budget ($000s)

	Quarter 1
Insurance Disbursements	
Variable items:	
Insurance claims	$ 3,697
Annuity benefits	1,755
Commissions	2,831
Total Variable Items	$ 8,283
Fixed items:	
Leases	$ 145
Payroll	1,134
General	705
Total Fixed Items	$ 1,984
Total Insurance Disbursements	$10,267
Investment Disbursements	
Short-term security purchases	$ 9,302
Long-term security purchases	1,601
Mortgage purchases	450
Total Investment Disbursements	$11,353
Total Cash Disbursements	$21,620

Insurers use many methods to derive the minimum cash balance. Most insurers set the minimum balance equal to the budgeted cash disbursements for one month. More sophisticated techniques involve computer spreadsheet simulations. By examining the cash budget, an insurer can estimate the timing and amount of cash shortages that will require short-term borrowing or the amount of excess cash that the insurer can invest in assets that can be readily converted into cash for an approximation of their true value. Figure 8-8 shows an example of a cash budget.

Capital Budgets

Capital budgeting is the process companies undertake to analyze decisions about investing in long-term projects or assets. Capital

FIGURE 8-8. A Cash Budget.

Quality's minimum cash balance for each quarter is $3,250,000. Quality expects that, by the end of the first quarter, it will encounter a cash shortage of $2,021,000. Quality has planned for a short-term loan in the amount of $2,500,000, which it expects to be able to repay, with interest, in the fourth quarter.

Cash Budget ($000s)

	Quarter				
	1	2	3	4	Total
Beginning Cash Balance	$ 4,020	$ 3,729	$ 9,210	$ 12,055	$ 4,020*
Total Cash Receipts	18,829	18,657	18,829	19,777	76,092
Total Cash Available (1)	$ 22,849	$22,386	$ 28,039	$ 31,832	$ 80,112 *
Cash disbursements:					
For insurance and annuities	$ 10,267	$ 9,923	$ 10,074	$ 10,387	$ 40,651
For investments	11,353	1,940	3,597	3,264	20,154
For computer equipment			1,001		1,001
Total Cash Disbursements (2)	$ 21,620	$11,863	$ 14,672	$13,651	$ 61,806
Minimum cash balance	3,250	3,250	3,250	3,250	3,250*
Total Cash Needed	$ 24,870	$15,113	$ 17,922	$16,901	$ 74,806
Excess (deficiency) of cash	$ (2,021)	$ 7,273	$ 10,117	$14,931	$ 5,306*
Short-term financing:					
Borrowing	$ 2,500				$ 2,500
Repayment		$ (1,250)	$ (1,250)		$ (2,500)
Interest (10% annually)		(63)	(62)		$ (125)
Total Effects of Financing (3)	$ 2,500	$ (1,313)	$ (1,312)	$ 0	$ (125)
Ending Cash Balance (1)–(2)+(3)	$ 3,729	$ 9,210	$12,055	$18,181	$ 18,181*

***Not a total of the monetary amounts in Quarters 1 through 4.**

budgeting often includes many steps, which are beyond the scope of this text. A ***capital budget*** shows a company's plans for the financial management of its long-term, high-cost investment proposals, such as new investments in equipment or real estate, major repairs to or remodeling of existing investments, acquisitions of other companies or lines of business, mandated safety and environmental improvements, expense reduction projects, and revenue expansion projects. A common trait of capital budgeting is that these investments are expected to produce income or other benefits for more than one year. Figure 8-9 presents an example of a capital budget for a proposed new facility.

Pro Forma Financial Statements

The master budget culminates in a set of pro forma financial statements. A ***pro forma financial statement*** projects what a company's financial condition will be at the end of an accounting period, assuming the company achieves all its goals. A set of pro forma statements includes a

- ***Pro forma income statement***, which estimates a company's net income. To prepare this statement, the company transfers the totals from each revenue budget and expense budget to the pro forma income statement. Managers use the pro forma income statement to obtain board approval and then monitor overall progress during the year.

FIGURE 8-9. A Capital Budget.

Design and Construction Summary Budget for a Proposed New Facility ($000s)	
Demolition	$ 70
General construction ($30.50 per square foot)	11,250
Mechanical	2,090
Electrical	1,577
Vertical transportation	875
Construction manager fee	428
Sitework (including landscaping and surface parking)	1,700
Parking deck	1,050
Renovation of existing building	1,100
Architect/engineers	1,000
Construction contingency reserve	650
Estimated Total	$21,790

- ***Pro forma cash flow statement***, which categorizes the company's budgeted cash receipts and cash disbursements into cash flows from: (1) operating activities, such as policy sales, benefit payments, and investment income; (2) investing activities, such as the purchase or sale of securities; and (3) financing activities, such as issuing stock, borrowing funds, or repaying a debt. The important monetary amount on a company's cash flow statement is the net increase or decrease in cash expected during the period. To prepare the pro forma cash flow statement, the company transfers financial information from the cash receipts and cash disbursements budgets, the cash budget, and the pro forma income statement to the pro forma cash flow statement.

- ***Pro forma balance sheet***, which predicts the change in asset, liability, and owners' equity accounts based on information contained in the master budget. The pro forma balance sheet assumes that the company's actual revenues and expenses equal its budgeted revenues and expenses. To prepare the pro forma balance sheet, the company incorporates changes that were made to the pro forma income statement and the pro forma cash flow statement.

Company managers compare actual and pro forma financial statements to determine whether the company has met its goals. Top management and the board of directors use variance analysis to evaluate the performance of the company and its management team. Figure 8-10 summarizes the budgeting process through relationships among the various components of a life insurer's master budget, including its pro forma financial statements.

FIGURE 8-10. Components of the Master Budget.

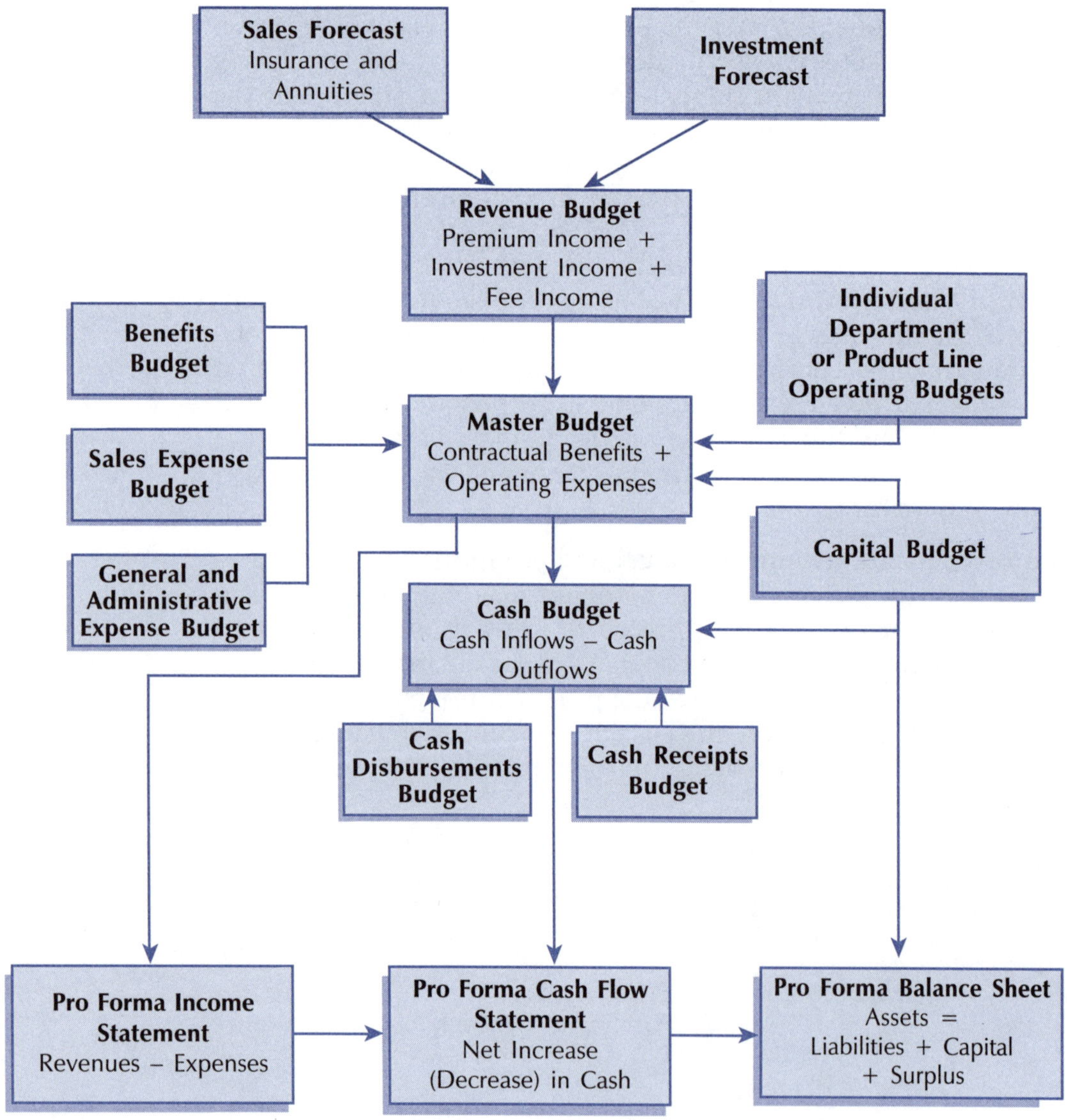

Key Terms and Concepts

budgeting
budget
top-down budgeting
bottom-up budgeting
zero-based budgeting (ZBB)
static budget
flexible budget
short-term budget
long-term budget
rolling budget
period budget
master budget
operational budgeting
operational budget
sales forecast
investment forecast
revenue budget
sales budget
investment budget
expense budget
benefits budget
sales expense budget
general and administrative expense budget
cash budgeting
cash budget
cash receipts budget
cash disbursements budget
minimum cash balance
line of credit
capital budgeting
capital budget
pro forma financial statement
pro forma income statement
pro forma cash flow statement
pro forma balance sheet

Glossary

ABC. *See* **activity-based costing (ABC).**

account. The basic tool that a company uses to record, group, and summarize similar types of financial transactions. [2]

accounting. A system or set of rules and methods for collecting, recording, summarizing, reporting, and analyzing a company's financial information. [1]

accounting controls. The policies and procedures used to authorize financial transactions, safeguard assets, and provide reliable, timely, and fairly presented financial information about a company. [4]

accounting entry. A record of a financial transaction that includes at least one debit and one credit that shows the monetary amount of the transaction. [2]

accrual-basis accounting. An accounting system in which a company records revenues when they are earned and expenses when they are incurred, even if the company has not yet received the revenues or paid the expenses. [3]

acquisition-cost concept. *See* **cost concept.**

activity. Any procedure that generates work, such as processing a policy application, sending a premium due notice, and investigating a claim. [7]

activity cost. The cost attributable to a specified activity, such as telephone charges in an insurer's customer service call center. [7]

activity driver. The output of an activity being performed; the purpose that propels the activity. [7]

activity-based costing (ABC). A type of costing that involves linking costs to products based on the activities consumed in producing the products or services. [7]

actuarial liabilities. *See* **reserves.**

adjusting entry. An accounting entry that a company makes to record internal financial transactions or correct errors that occur in one or more accounting periods. [2]

administrative controls. The policies and procedures that guide employees in conducting their normal day-to-day tasks. [4]

adverse opinion. An auditor's opinion stating that the financial statements do not fairly present the entity's financial condition. [4]

AICPA. *See* **American Institute of Certified Public Accountants (AICPA).**

allocation base. A measure of use that exhibits a proportional relationship between indirect costs and the cost center being allocated a portion of those costs. [6]

American Institute of Certified Public Accountants (AICPA). A professional association of U.S. Certified Public Accountants (CPAs) that directly influences accounting practice in the United States in a variety of ways, including the development of generally accepted auditing standards (GAAS). [1]

Annual Return. In Canada, a document that presents information about an insurer's operations and financial performance, with an emphasis on demonstrating the insurer's solvency and profitability. [1]

Annual Statement. In the United States, a document that presents information about an insurer's operations and financial performance, with an emphasis on demonstrating the insurer's solvency. [1]

assets. The account classification that represents all items, generally, of readily determinable monetary value that a company owns. [2]

associating cause and effect. An expense recognition concept which states that expenses that have a direct relationship to specified future revenues are charged to future accounting periods instead of being charged to the current accounting period. [3]

audit. An evaluation of whether a company's financial information, financial statements, and source documents comply with accounting standards and are a fair and consistent depiction of the company's financial condition and performance. [4]

audit trail. A chronological, sequential set of accounting records and reports from the beginning to the end of a business transaction. [4]

auditor's opinion. A statement, prepared by an independent public accounting company, that attests that the information contained in a company's annual report fairly represents the operations of the company and that the audit was conducted in accordance with generally accepted auditing standards (GAAS). [4]

authorization level. The maximum monetary amount that a company employee has been granted official power to approve for disbursing company expenditures. [4]

balance sheet. A financial statement that shows an insurer's financial condition or position as of a specified date [1]

balance sheet equation. *See* **basic accounting equation.**

bank line. *See* **line of credit.**

base period. The earliest financial reporting period used in horizontal analysis. [7]

basic accounting equation. Presents the relationship among the three key account classifications—assets, liabilities, and owners' equity—on the balance sheet. [2]

benchmarking. An analytical process wherein an insurer selects a number of other companies to use as a "best-practices" standard for comparison with the company's own operations and expenses. [7]

benefits budget. A budget that indicates the amount of money the insurer expects to pay for claims, cash surrenders, and policy dividends during the next accounting period. [8]

book value. The value at which an asset is recorded in a company's accounting records. [3]

bottom-up budgeting. A budgeting process that is generated in each department or responsibility center by lower-level managers and is presented in the form of recommendations to senior management. [8]

breakeven analysis. *See* **cost-volume-profit analysis.**

breakeven chart. *See* **cost-volume-profit graph.**

breakeven point. The point at which a product's total revenues equal its total costs and the product's fixed costs equal its contribution margin. [7]

budget. A financial plan of action, expressed in monetary terms, which covers a specified time period, such as one year. *See also* **master budget.** [8]

budgeting. A management accounting process that includes creating a financial plan of action that an organization believes will help achieve its goals. [8]

Canada Customs and Revenue Agency. The governmental agency—formerly known as Revenue Canada—responsible for enforcing the provisions of Canadian laws and regulations concerning income taxes. [1]

Canadian Institute of Chartered Accountants (CICA). A professional organization of Canadian Chartered Accountants (CAs) that establishes Canadian GAAP for insurers to follow in recording and presenting their financial information. [1]

capital. Items that represent the money that a company's owners have invested in the company. [2]

capital budget. A budget that shows a company's plans for the financial management of its long-term, high-cost investment proposals, such as new investments in equipment or real estate, major repairs to or remodeling of existing investments, acquisitions of other companies or lines of business, mandated safety and environmental improvements, expense reduction projects, and revenue expansion projects. [8]

capital budgeting. The process companies undertake to analyze decisions about investing in long-term projects or assets. [8]

cash budget. A type of budget that projects a company's beginning cash balance, cash inflows, cash outflows, and ending cash balance for a specified accounting period, typically by quarter. [8]

cash budgeting. A budgeting activity that anticipates the cash flows into and out of a company during an accounting period. [8]

cash disbursement. The payment of cash by a company to a beneficiary or other payee. [3]

cash disbursements budget. A schedule of expected cash disbursements, including their timing and amount, during the accounting period. [8]

cash flow statement. A financial statement that provides information about an insurer's cash receipts (inflows) and its cash disbursements (outflows) during a specified period. [1]

cash receipt. A check, money order, electronic funds transfer (EFT), or other cash transaction that is remitted to a company as a form of payment for goods or services rendered. [3]

cash receipts budget. A schedule of cash receipts expected during the accounting period. [8]

cash-basis accounting. An accounting system in which a company recognizes revenues or expenses only when it receives or disburses cash. [3]

chargeback. A cost allocation method under which a department allocates its indirect costs to departments based on usage. [6]

chart of accounts. A numbered or alphabetical list of all the company's account names. [2]

CICA. *See* **Canadian Institute of Chartered Accountants.**

clean opinion. *See* **unqualified opinion.**

closing entry. An accounting entry that a company makes at the end of each accounting period to start the next accounting period with a zero balance in its temporary accounts. [2]

codification. The process undertaken to help standardize financial reporting requirements among the 50 states. [1]

collusion. A secret agreement entered into by two or more persons to perpetrate an illegal act. [4]

committed cost. A cost that results from a prior management decision and that cannot be changed quickly. [6]

common cost. *See* **indirect cost.**

common-size financial statement. A financial statement that consists of the percentages obtained from vertical analysis. [7]

comparability. The quality of accounting information that requires a company's financial statements to be presented in such a way that interested users can identify similarities and differences in financial information across accounting periods and among different companies. [3]

comparative financial statements. Financial statements that present data for two or more accounting periods. [7]

compliance audit. A type of audit that verifies that an insurer's financial statements adhere to the laws, regulations, policies, and procedures prescribed by internal and external regulatory authorities. [4]

compound accounting entry. A record of a financial transaction that affects more than two accounts. [2]

comprehensive budget. *See* **master budget.**

comptroller. *See* **controller.**

conservatism. The quality of accounting information that requires a prudent reaction for dealing with uncertainty in accounting records and reports; in practice, the use of conservatism typically understates the values of a company's assets and revenues and overstates the values of the company's liabilities and expenses. [3]

consistency. The quality of accounting information that requires a company to use the same accounting policies and procedures in its financial statements from one accounting period to the next, unless there is a sound reason for changing a specified policy or procedure. [3]

continuous budget. *See* **rolling budget.**

contribution margin. The difference between a product's selling price and its variable costs. [7]

contribution margin ratio. A measure of segment performance, calculated by dividing the contribution margin by the segment's total revenues. [7]

controllable cost. A cost over which a responsibility manager has decision-making authority. [5]

controller. The head of a company's accounting function. [1]

corporate budget. *See* **master budget.**

corporate planning. *See* **strategic planning.**

cost accounting. A system for accumulating expense data used to facilitate effective cost control and accurate estimates of future costs for use in the pricing of a company's products. [6]

cost accumulation. The process of capturing all company costs and categorizing them in meaningful ways. [6]

cost allocation. The accounting process of assigning or distributing an indirect cost (expense) according to a specified method or formula. [5]

cost center. A department or other business segment to which costs (expenses) can be traced. [5]

cost concept. An accounting principle which states that companies should include items on the balance sheet and income statement according to their actual cost at the time of purchase. [3]

cost object. Any purpose for which a company measures costs. [5]

cost-volume-profit (CVP) analysis. The study of the effects of changes in product prices, sales volume, fixed costs, variable costs, and the type of products a company offers. [7]

cost-volume-profit (CVP) graph. A graph that highlights relationships among cost, volume, and profit over a wide range of sales levels. [7]

credit. In an accounting entry, a specified change that increases the monetary value of liability accounts, owners' equity accounts, and revenue accounts, or decreases the monetary value of asset accounts and expense accounts. [2]

current market value. The price at which an asset can be sold under current economic conditions. [3]

CVP analysis. *See* **cost-volume-profit analysis.**

CVP graph. *See* **cost-volume-profit graph.**

debit. In an accounting entry, a specified change that increases the monetary value of asset accounts and expense accounts, or decreases the monetary value of liability accounts, owners' equity accounts, and revenue accounts. [2]

decision making. The process of identifying and selecting a course of action to solve a problem or take advantage of an opportunity. [5]

depreciation. The process of spreading (allocating) the cost of an asset over the asset's estimated useful life. [3]

detective control. An internal control that identifies an error or problem after it has occurred. [4]

differential cost. A cost that changes as a result of a future decision. [6]

direct cost. A cost incurred for or physically traceable to one specific product, line of business, department, or other cost object. [5]

direct method. A cost allocation method that assumes that a service department benefits production departments only. [6]

disclaimer (denial) of opinion. An auditor's opinion which indicates that the external auditor has no opinion on the financial statements of the entity. [4]

discretionary cost. A cost that results from periodic management decisions that change as conditions change. [6]

double-entry accounting. The accounting function that tracks and reports an insurer's transactions, in which (1) every financial transaction has at least one debit and one credit, (2) the total monetary amount of the debits must equal that of the credits for each transaction, and (3) each accounting entry must maintain the balance of the basic accounting equation. [2]

dual concept. An accounting concept that states that every financial transaction has two aspects—debits and credits—that always equal each other. [2]

dual control. *See* **segregation of duties.**

dynamic budget. *See* **flexible budget.**

entity. The basic business unit for which a company keeps separate accounting records and reports. [3]

entity concept. An accounting principle that states that a company must account separately for the business activities of each business unit. [3]

execution of transactions as authorized. The element of the internal control system that concerns the delegation of authority to perform specified tasks and the communication of that authority. [4]

expense budget. A schedule of expenses expected during an accounting period. [8]

expenses. The account classification that represents the amount of one or more assets that a company uses to receive a certain benefit or service. [2]

external audit. A type of internal control that is performed by external auditors, employed by public accounting firms or insurance regulators, who assess and evaluate the company's internal controls. [4]

fair market value. *See* **current market value.**

FASB. *See* **Financial Accounting Standards Board.**

favorable variance. A variance in which the standard cost is higher than the actual cost. [6]

fidelity bond. An indemnity insurance agreement guaranteeing to the purchaser the coverage of a financial loss caused by (1) the act or default of a third party, such as an employee, or (2) some contingency, such as fire, over which the third party may have no control. (4)

Financial Accounting Standards Board (FASB). A private organization, funded by the accounting profession and companies with an interest in accounting practices, that establishes and promotes the use of generally accepted accounting principles (GAAP) in the United States. [1]

financial accounting. A field of accounting that focuses primarily on reporting a company's financial information to meet the needs of the company's external users. [1]

financial auditing. The process of examining and evaluating company records and procedures to ensure that (1) the company's accounting records and financial statements are presented fairly and reasonably, (2) quality assurance is maintained, and (3) operational procedures and policies are effective. [4]

financial statements. Standardized reports of a company's major monetary events and transactions. [1]

financial transaction. A business transaction to which a company must assign an objective monetary value, whether the impact on the company is large or small, actual or expected. [1]

fiscal year. A 12-month accounting period chosen by a company for financial reporting purposes. [3]

fixed budget. *See* **static budget.**

fixed cost. A cost that remains constant for all levels of operating activity or production. [6]

fixed-amount budget. *See* **static budget.**

flexible budget. A budget that provides alternative sets of budget estimates to use under the different circumstances that may arise during an accounting period. [8]

flexible-amount budget. *See* **flexible budget.**

fraud. The intentional use of false information to mislead another party. [4]

full-disclosure concept. An accounting principle which states that a company's financial statements must contain all material information about the company and that the company must disclose any additional information or fact that, by its omission, could mislead an interested user of the company's financial information. [3]

function. A series of activities that serve a specific purpose. [6]

functional cost analysis. A subset of activity-based costing that involves the process of accumulating the costs that are involved in each activity within a function. [7]

functional costs. The accumulated costs of the activities involved within a certain function, without regard to organizational units. [6]

functional unit cost. A type of functional cost that is calculated by dividing the total functional cost by an appropriate base unit. [7]

functional-area planning. The process of creating long-term plans for various functional areas of a company. [5]

GAAP. *See* **generally accepted accounting principles.**

general and administrative expense budget. A budget that includes expenses—typically fixed expenses—needed for insurance company operations. [8]

generally accepted accounting principles (GAAP). A set of financial accounting standards that all public companies in the United States and all companies in Canada follow when preparing their financial statements. [1]

going-concern concept. An accounting principle that requires a company's accounting records to reflect the assumption that the company will continue to operate indefinitely. [3]

historical cost. The original purchase price of an asset. [3]

historical-cost concept. *See* **cost concept.**

horizontal analysis. A type of financial statement analysis that involves calculating the absolute amount and the percentage of the increase or decrease in a specified financial statement from one reporting period to another. [7]

IASC. *See* **International Accounting Standards Committee.**

immediate recognition. An expense recognition concept, common under statutory reporting requirements, which states that a company recognize all costs as expenses during the current accounting period. [3]

income statement. A financial statement that reports an insurer's profits or losses by summarizing the insurer's revenues and expenses during a specified period. [1]

incompatible functions. Job duties that, when combined, place an employee in a position to commit an illegal act or to conceal errors or irregularities in the normal course of his or her employment. [4]

incremental cost. *See* **marginal cost.**

index number. In trend analysis, a number that provides a statistical method for measuring the change in a variable. [7]

index-number trend analysis. *See* **trend analysis.**

indirect cost. A cost that is not incurred for or cannot be physically traced to one specific cost object. [5]

initial-recording concept. *See* **cost concept.**

internal audit. A type of internal control that is performed by company employees who assess and evaluate the company's internal controls. [4]

internal control. The steps a company takes to (1) protect its assets, (2) monitor the accuracy of its accounting records, and (3) encourage both operational efficiency and adherence to the company's management policies. [4]

Internal Revenue Service (IRS). A part of the U.S. Department of the Treasury, the governmental agency responsible for enforcing the provisions of laws and regulations concerning income taxes in the United States. [1]

International Accounting Standards Committee (IASC). An organization charged with promulgating accounting standards that are applicable internationally, independent of the home country of a company's financial statements. [1]

inventory. An itemized count and listing of a company's assets, such as property, products, materials, or securities. [4]

investable funds. Consist of (1) net income before taxes, (2) investment income received on prior investments, and (3) the maturities of principal on prior investments. [5]

investment budget. A budget that projects the types of investments the insurer will make and the expected amount of investment income for each type of investment. [8]

investment center. A department or other business segment to which costs (expenses), revenues, and capital or investment funds can be traced. [5]

investment forecast. An estimate of the performance, for a specified period, of bonds, stocks, mortgages, and other invested assets a company owns. [8]

investment segmentation method. An investment income allocation method under which an insurer uses the cash flows of a product line or line of business to purchase specific investments for that line. [5]

investment year method. An investment income allocation method that forms separate investment pools containing the investments made during each year, thus overcoming one weakness of the mean liabilities method. [5]

IRS. *See* **Internal Revenue Service.**

journal entry. *See* **accounting entry.**

liabilities. The account classification that represents a company's monetary value for its current and future obligations. [2]

line of business. A segment of products that has a cost pattern distinct from that of other product segments. [6]

line of credit. A prearranged agreement whereby a company can borrow money for a short-term, up to a specified amount. [8]

liquidation. The process of selling all company or entity assets, usually to pay of liabilities. [3]

liquidity. The ease with which an asset can be converted to cash with little or no loss in value. [2]

long-term assets. Assets that a company plans to hold indefinitely or for a long time—generally more than a year—to generate income. [2]l

long-term budget. A budget, generally covering periods of more than one year, that allows a company to estimate revenues and expenses that correspond to the companys strategic goals. [8]

long-term liabilities. Financial obligations that do not have to be paid in full during the current accounting period—usually one year. [2]

management accounting. The process of identifying, measuring, analyzing, and communicating financial information. [1]

management audit. A type of performance audit that focuses on improving the effectiveness and efficiency of an insurer's operations. [4]

management by exception (MBE). A principle stating that managers should be informed about operational progress only when a result or activity differs by a specified monetary amount or percentage from what was expected. [5]

margin. In the context of contribution margin, the excess of a product's revenues over its costs. [7]

marginal cost. The additional total expense incurred as a result of producing one additional unit of an existing product or service. [6]

marginal unit cost. The increase or decrease in the unit cost as a result of an additional unit of a good or service. [6]

market value. *See* **current market value.**

master budget. The overall operating and financing plans for the company during a specified accounting period. *See* also **budget.** [8]

matching principle. A GAAP expense recognition concept which states that a company should recognize expenses as the company earns the revenues related to those expenses, regardless of when the company receives payment for the revenues earned. [3]

materiality. The quality of accounting information that requires companies to disclose all significant information in their financial statements. [3]

MBE. *See* **management by exception.**

mean liabilities method. An investment income allocation method that allocates investment income to lines of business on the basis of the reserves that are attributable to each line. [5]

measuring-unit concept. An accounting principle which states that a company should record its accounting information in monetary terms, such as U.S. dollars or Canadian dollars. [3]

minimum cash balance. The amount of cash that an insurer determines is necessary to pay all obligations in an accounting period without having excess cash. [8]

mixed cost. *See* **semi-variable cost.**

modified opinion. An auditor's opinion that contains explanatory language concerning specified circumstances, such as material inconsistencies resulting from a change in accounting principles or practices. [4]

modified unqualified consistency report. *See* **modified opinion.**

NAIC. *See* **National Association of Insurance Commissioners.**

National Association of Insurance Commissioners (NAIC). An association of state insurance commissioners designed to promote consistent insurance regulation. [1]

negative variance. A variance in which the actual amount or percentage of an amount is less than expected, which is favorable for expense items and unfavorable for revenue items. [5]

net gain from operations. A gain that results if a company's operating revenues exceed its operating expenses. [2]

net income. The excess of a company's total revenues over total expenses. [2]

net loss. The excess of a company's total expenses over total revenues. [2]

net loss from operations. A loss that results if a company's operating expenses exceed its operating revenues. [2]

nominal account. *See* **temporary account.**

noncontrollable cost. A cost over which a responsibility manager has no decision-making authority. [5]

non-value-added activity. An activity that does not make a product or service more valuable to the customer. [7]

normal balance. Whether a debit or a credit to the account increases the account's monetary value. [2]

Office of the Superintendent of Financial Institutions (OSFI). The Canadian government agency primarily responsible for overseeing federally registered insurance companies in Canada and ensuring their compliance with federal laws and regulations. [1]

operating budget. *See* **short-term budget.**

operating cycle. The way in which funds flow through a company as it conducts its day-to-day business activities. [2]

operating department. *See* **production department.**

operating expenses. The expenses that a company incurs in conducting its normal business operations. [2]

operational budget. A budget that includes part or all a company's core business operations. [8]

operational budgeting. A budgeting activity that covers all or part of a company's operations. [8]

operational planning. The process of determining how to accomplish specified tasks with available resources, given a company's strategic plan. [5]

opportunity cost. The benefit that is forfeited or given up in choosing one decision alternative over another. [6]

OSFI. *See* **Office of the Superintendent of Financial Institutions (OSFI).**

out-of-pocket cost. A cost that requires outlays of cash or other resources. [6]

overhead expenses. Costs, incurred during normal business operations, that are not directly associated with a specified product or service. [5]

owners' equity. The account classification that represents the owners' investment in a company. [2]

performance audit. A type of audit that measures and evaluates progress toward achieving management objectives for a particular function or goals. [4]

performance plan. *See* **master budget.**

period budget. A budget that covers a specific time frame, such as one month or one year, and expires at the end of that time frame. [8]

permanent account. A balance sheet account that has a monetary balance at the beginning of each accounting period. [2]

physical comparison of recorded amounts. The accounting principle that requires a company to count its assets, revenues, and expenses and compare this count to the amounts in its accounting records on a periodic basis. [4]

policy dividend. The portion of an insurer's surplus that is paid to the policyowner of a participating policy. [2]

positive variance. A variance in which the actual amount or percentage of an amount is greater than expected, and it is considered favorable for revenue items and unfavorable for expense items. [5]

predictive quality. A characteristic of accounting information that enables interested users to form a reasonably accurate estimate of a company's financial strength or earnings potential. [3]

premium income. The income that an insurer receives for assuming the financial risk associated with a specified loss. [2]

preventive control. An internal control that is designed to keep an error or a problem from occurring. [4]

pro forma balance sheet. A financial statement that predicts the change in asset, liability, and owners' equity accounts based on information contained in the company's master budget. [8]

pro forma cash flow statement. A financial statement that categorizes the company's budgeted cash receipts and cash disbursements into cash flows from: (1) operating activities, (2) investing activities, and (3) financing activities. [8]

pro forma financial statement. A financial statement that projects what a company's financial condition will be at the end of an accounting period, assuming the company achieves all its goals.

pro forma income statement. A financial statement that estimates a company's net income. [8]

production department. A department that engages in an insurance company's revenue-generating activities. [6]

profit center. A department or other business segment to which both costs (expenses) and revenues can be traced. [5]

profit plan. *See* **master budget.**

profitability. The degree to which a company is successful in consistently generating money for its owners. [1]

profit-volume analysis. *See* **cost-volume-profit analysis.**

program results audit. A type of performance audit that determines whether the desired results or benefits are actually being achieved under a specified program. [4]

qualified opinion. An auditor's opinion that states the area of exception to an otherwise unqualified opinion: for example, an insurer has a large pending lawsuit for a disputed claim for which the amount of the claim liability is material and under contention. [4]

rate variance. The difference between a product's actual rate (or unit cost or price) and the rate budgeted for that product, multiplied by the actual number of units sold or processed. [5]

realization principle. A GAAP revenue recognition concept which states that a company should recognize revenue when it is earned, regardless of when the company receives the actual payment, so long as a legal and reasonable expectation exists that the customer will remit payment in full. [3]

reciprocal method. A cost allocation method that fully recognizes the services that service departments perform for each other. [6]

recognition. The process of classifying an item in a financial statement as an asset, liability, owners' equity, revenue, or expense. [3]

recording of transactions as executed. A company records all authorized and executed transactions in the correct accounting period, in the correct accounts, and in the correct monetary amounts. [4]

relevance. The quality of accounting information that requires a company's accounting information to be useful, timely, and likely to affect an interested user's decisions. [3]

reliability. The quality of accounting information that requires a company's accounting records and financial statements to present accurate, objective information that is free from bias and misrepresentation. [3]

reserves. Liability accounts that identify the amounts of money that an insurer expects to need to meet its future contractual obligations. [2]

responsibility accounting. A people-oriented system of policies and procedures that allows for revenues, expenses, and investments to be assigned to a specified employee or organizational level that is accountable for those specific revenues, expenses, and investments. [5]

responsibility center. The area, function, or organizational unit that a specified manager controls. [5]

responsibility center report. *See* **responsibility report.**

responsibility report. A management accounting report that itemizes budgeted and actual amounts that are under the responsibility manager's sphere of control and the corresponding variance for each revenue or cost (expense). [5]

retained earnings. A GAAP account that represents the cumulative amount of a company's earnings that has been kept in the company over time to finance the company's ongoing operations. [2]

revenue budget. A budget that indicates the amount of income from operations—policy sales and investments—that the company expects in the coming budget period. [8]

Revenue Canada. *See* **Canada Customs and Revenue Agency.**

revenues. The account classification that represents the amounts earned from a company's core business operations. [2]

rolling budget. A budget that allows a company to continually maintain projections for a specified time period into the future. [8]

safeguarding of assets. The process of (1) limiting access to offices, documents, and records; (2) storing negotiable documents in vaults to which no person has sole access; (3) maintaining written business disaster recovery plans and off-premises storage of back-up files for all critical records; (4) investigating the integrity of employees hired to fill sensitive position; (5) taking a physical inventory of all assets and comparing this count to a written record; and (6) reviewing the adequacy of insurance coverage, given a company's risk exposure. [4]

sales budget. A budget that projects first-year and renewal premium income. [8]

sales expense budget. A budget that indicates the costs incurred in selling insurance. [8]

sales forecast. An estimate of insurance and annuity sales for a particular period. [8]

salvage value. The residual value or selling price of an asset at the end of its useful life. [3]

SAPs. *See* **statutory accounting practices.**

SEC. *See* **Securities and Exchange Commission.**

Securities and Exchange Commission (SEC). A federal government agency that regulates the investment industry in the United States. [1]

segment. A product, line of business, or responsibility center. [7]

segment margin. The portion of the contribution margin that remains after a segment has covered its direct fixed costs. [7]

segment margin ratio. A measure of a segment's efficiency of operating performance, calculated by dividing the segment margin by the segment's total revenues. [7]

segment report. A type of management accounting report that shows revenues and expenses for a single responsibility center. [5]

segregation of duties. The accounting principle that requires an employer to design jobs so that incompatible functions are assigned to different individuals. [4]

semi-variable cost. A cost that is comprised of a fixed cost component plus the amount of a variable component over time and at each volume level. [6]

service department. A department that provides support services to production departments and to other service departments but does not itself generate revenue. [6]

shared cost. *See* **indirect cost.**

short-term assets. Assets that a company expects to readily convert into cash or consume within the current accounting period, typically one year. [2]

short-term budget. A budget that generally covers a period of one year or less and relates mainly to a company's operations during that period. [8]

short-term liabilities. Financial obligations that must be paid in one year or less. [2]

simple accounting entry. A record of a financial transaction that affects only two accounts, and thus has only one debit and one credit. [2]

simultaneous method. *See* **reciprocal method.**

solvency. The ability of a company to meet its financial obligations as they come due. [1]

source documents. The various business papers and electronic forms that contain original information about a company's financial transactions. [2]

standard audit opinion. An auditor's opinion indicating that the financial statements present fairly, in all material respects, the financial position, results of operations, and changes in financial position of the entity in accordance with Canadian GAAP. [4]

standard cost. A predetermined cost expected to be incurred for particular items during normal business operations. [6]

standard report. *See* **unqualified opinion.**

statement of owners' equity. A financial statement that shows the changes that occurred in an insurer's stockholders' equity or policyowners' equity during a specified period [1]

static budget. A budget that contains amounts that are generally not subject to change unless management has approved the changes. [8]

statutory accounting practices (SAPs). The accounting standards that all life insurers in the United States must follow when preparing the Annual Statement and specified other financial reports that are submitted to regulators. [1]

step method. A cost allocation method that assumes that service departments perform services for production departments and for other service departments. [6]

step-down allocation. *See* **step method.**

strategic budget. *See* **long-term budget.**

strategic planning. The process of determining how to pursue comprehensive, organization-wide, long-term goals with available resources. [5]

sunk cost. A cost that does not change as a result of a future decision. [6]

surplus. Under statutory accounting practices, the cumulative monetary amount that remains in an insurance company over time. [2]

systematic and rational allocation. An expense recognition concept which states that a company expenses an asset's cost over its estimated useful life, regardless of when the company receives revenues from the asset. [3]

temporary account. An account that is zeroed out to a permanent account on the balance sheet at the end of each accounting period. [2]

time analysis. A method of allocating indirect salary costs by determining the percentage of time a manager spends with different departments or activities. [6]

time-period concept. An accounting principle stating that a company's financial statements should report the company's business operations during a specified time period, usually referred to as an accounting period. [3]

top-down budgeting. A budgeting process that begins with a company's senior management and is passed down to lower-level management. [8]

transfer price. The price of a good or service that one business segment or line of business charges another segment or line of the same company. [5]

trend. A change that occurs over time. [7]

trend analysis. A type of horizontal analysis that involves calculating percentage changes in financial statement items over more than two successive accounting periods. [7]

trend percentages. *See* **trend analysis.**

unfavorable variance. A variance in which the actual cost is higher than the standard cost. [6]

unit cost. The incurred expense attributable to a single measured amount of work. [6]

unqualified opinion. An auditor's opinion stating that the financial statements present fairly, in all material respects, the financial position, results of operations, and cash flows of the entity in conformity with GAAP or, for "special purpose" financial statements, in accordance with statutory accounting practices. [4]

usage variance. The difference between the actual quantities to be sold or processed and the budgeted quantities sold or processed, multiplied by the budgeted rate. [5]

value-added activity. An activity that makes a product or service more valuable to the customer. [7]

variable budget. *See* **flexible budget.**

variable cost. A cost that changes in direct response to changes in the level of operating activity. [6]

variance. The difference whenever an actual result differs from an assumed or expected result. [5]

variance analysis. The study of the difference between expected or assumed results and actual results. [5]

vertical analysis. A type of financial statement analysis that reveals the relationship of each financial statement item to a specified financial statement item during the same reporting period. [7]

volume. In the context of cost-volume-profit analysis, the quantity of sales that is associated with the product being analyzed. [7]

ZBB. *See* **zero-based budgeting.**

zero-based budgeting (ZBB). A budgeting process in which a company begins with the premise that no resources will be allocated for the next accounting period unless and until each expense is shown to be in accord with the company's strategic and operational goals. [8]

Index

An *f* following a page number indicates a Figure or Insight.

A

B

C

K

L

M

N

O

P

T

U

V–Y

Z